WHAT DO YOU SEE?

WHAT DO YOU SEE?

A DEVOTIONAL JOURNAL

PHYLLIS SWEITZER

FOREWORD BY HARRIET Z. MAUER, DD

What Do You See?
Total Fusion Ministries
Ohio, USA

Editing and interior design by Kara Starcher of mountaincreekbooks.com

ISBN (paperback): 978-1-943496-24-2

To the love of my life, Don.
You have stood beside me and supported me all of our days.
You have been a gift in my life.
I will love you forever.

To my children, Sarah and Kyle.
My life was made complete when I became your mother.
I still thank God every day for the blessing of you in my life.

To my children's spouses, Jessica and Adam.
My children chose very well. Thank you for loving them and
for giving me grandchildren.

To my grandchildren, Abbey, Natalee, Charlie, Hannah, and Owen.
You are all the icing on the cake.
I love each of you so much and
pray that you will always
see Jesus in your life.

FOREWORD

by Harriet Z. Mouer, DD

WELCOME TO THE WORLD of my friend Phyllis Sweitzer. You will not read this book. You will encounter it! That's because it seems to have a heartbeat that makes her stories come alive.

I have known Phyllis for about twenty-five years. Our first meeting was when we each were involved in women's ministries at our local churches in Ohio. Periodically, we chatted at conferences and shared about the joys and some tough places too in women's lives and how we both desired to see God bring them into places of personal renewal and awakening.

After I received training as a Lifeforming Leadership Coach, Phyllis asked if I would coach her regarding her role she held for many years in a legal office. Our conversations led her to a decision that brought about the beginning of a retirement transition with the timing being just right to begin her ministry role at her local church.

It was during those sessions when I began to love Phyllis as a sister, to honor her as a gifted leader, and to deeply respect the high calling evident in her life.

Both Phyllis and I have the same appreciation for those who have been our pastors and spiritual leaders who sponsored us for positions in church ministry. We both are grateful for their influence that has prompted us to see God's unique vision for our own lives. And they know who they are, including our husbands!

As you experience this book, I believe you will find God validating His life in you. At times you will love daydreaming about how thoughtful God has been. Your eyes will be opened to realize His personal attentive care, whether you are reading about being refreshed as you are thinking about the dew on the grass, or her "snowbird" neighbors returning from Florida after a cold winter they missed in Ohio, or laughing out loud at the funniest story!

Sometimes she will refer to looking out her window in her study and noticing the tiniest element that gives her a uniquely different perspective about something we would probably ignore.

Ever feel like you are caught in a web? Perfect! You will love that entry! And sometimes, Phyllis will tenderly share some of her own trials that were obviously heavy, humanly weakening, and without hope. Until…

Another part I also love is journaling what God is bringing alive to my own heart as I read the stories. And to those who do not journal, Phyllis makes it super easy—so easy that you will want to grab a pen and start writing. Her questions are thoughtful and uniquely designed to help us with life-challenging insights. So, whether you write a few words or need more space for all your thoughts, you engage the heart of *What Do You See?* (WDYS).

Maybe, like Phyllis, you have a window where you enjoy seeing what's happening on the outside of your home. Reading this book just might launch you to have more of your own WDYS experiences.

Thanks, Phyllis!

Harriet Z. Mouer, DD
Lifeforming Leadership Coach
Charlotte, North Carolina
October 2024

Introduction
WDYS—What Do You See?

WHAT DO YOU SEE when you look at a sunflower? Are you like me who at times barely glances at it and moves on? Or perhaps you really look at it and comprehend its intricate design and beauty, noticing the veins of each petal, finding yourself amazed that the center is made up of hundreds of flowers? There is also the vibrant yellow contrasted against the dark center. And, like on the cover, there just might be a bee in the center drinking of its nectar. This amazing flower is here for a purpose and is a masterpiece of design that we are privileged to experience every summer.

Do you have a tendency of living life and just going through the motions, which for most of us is typical?

How about noticing what is around you?

Oh, to really *see* and comprehend! How often do we just pass through to the next activity or responsibility without noticing our surroundings?

Noticing nature…ah, the beauty! Do we really pay attention to the sky, trees, flowers, insects, birds, or wildlife?

How about people? Do we look at the faces of the cashiers in the store or the servers at the restaurant? Do we look into their eyes? Or notice their countenance?

Here is the big question for us. How do we see God? Where does He fit? Or maybe He doesn't fit? Really seeing God is about not having limitations regarding His presence. And that may be a challenge. Or maybe not! Let's keep talking about that…

In John we read about Thomas who wanted to see before He believed.

Seeing is what caused Thomas to accept that Jesus had been resurrected and was alive.

John 20:24–29 NKJV

24 Now Thomas, called the Twin, one of the twelve, was not with them when Jesus came. 25 The other disciples therefore said to him, "We have seen the Lord."

So he said to them, "Unless I see in His hands the print of the nails, and put my finger into the print of the nails, and put my hand into His side, I will not believe."

26 And after eight days His disciples were again inside, and Thomas with them. Jesus came, the doors being shut, and stood in the midst, and said, "Peace to you!" 27 Then He said to Thomas, "Reach your finger here, and look at My hands; and reach your hand here, and put it into My side. Do not be unbelieving, but believing."

28 And Thomas answered and said to Him, "My Lord and my God!"

29 Jesus said to him, "Thomas, because you have seen Me, you have believed. Blessed are those who have not seen and yet have believed."

My prayer is that as you read through these daily devotionals you will begin to see God in a new way. He is not just Jesus on paper; He is so much more. When we actually see Him, we begin to understand His greatness.

The Foundation

IN JEREMIAH 1, GOD asked Jeremiah what he saw twice. Both times Jeremiah told God what he saw, and God confirmed that he was seeing correctly. God then began revealing His plan to Jeremiah. God really wants us to see Him.

A couple of years ago I was challenged by my pastor to see Jesus in a new way, to notice him in little things. Jesus began asking me WDYS (*What Do You See?*). I would look, and He would show me that He was everywhere and in everything. I then began my journey of looking for Him in places I had never seen Him before.

Romans 11:36 NLT

For everything comes from Him and exists
by his power and is intended for his glory.
All glory to him forever! Amen.

John 1:3 NIV

Through him all things were made; without
him nothing was made that has been made.

Colossians 1:16 NLT

For through Him God created everything
in the heavenly realms and on earth.
He made the things we can see
and the things we can't see—
such as thrones, kingdoms, rulers, and au-

thorities in the unseen world. Everything
was created through him and for him.

This journey has proven to my heart that these verses are absolutely true. Daily, God shows me the little things and applies them to my life. This process is very important to my understanding of who He is.

The purpose of this book is to share my experiences with you in the hope that you too will begin to *see* Him in everything and give Him the worship (worth ship) that belongs only to Him. As you read each day, please spend time meditating, asking Him to show Himself to you. Will you please use the space provided to journal what you are being shown by your heavenly Father?

DAY ONE

Cobwebs
WDYS

TODAY, WHEN I LOOKED out my window, Jesus asked me WDYS. As I look, I see a cobweb hanging in the maple tree just outside the window of my study. The dew still clinging to it shows off its perfectly symmetrical and beautiful form. The sun shining through it enhances its intricate design. God designed that spider with creative abilities. The spider doesn't know that he's creative; he just does what he is designed to do.

As I thought about the cobweb, I realized that the animal kingdom and the natural kingdom, i.e., trees, flowers, rain, rivers, etc., are all obedient to their Creator. The seasons obediently do the work that God created for them. The flowers bloom in the spring and summer. The weather is appropriate to the current season bringing rain and snow as necessary. The winds freshen the air and move the weather. The sun brings daylight and warms the earth. The moon gives light to the night. Everything around us performs as designed by God, with one exception.

That exception is mankind. Yes, you and me. Man, though created by God, is disobedient. All who have gone before us and all who will follow are disobedient to God because of the fall and disobedience of Adam and Eve. We now live in a fallen world and are subjected to sin and the consequences of sin in our daily lives.

Genesis 3:11–13 NLT

¹¹ "Who told you that you were naked?" the
LORD God asked. "Have you eaten from the

tree whose fruit I commanded you not to eat?"

¹² The man replied, "It was the woman you gave me who gave me the fruit, and I ate it."

¹³ Then the LORD God asked the woman, "What have you done?"

"The serpent deceived me," she replied. "That's why I ate it."

What is God showing you about obedience today? Take a moment and journal what He is showing you. WDYS?

_____

_____

_____

_____

_____

_____

_____

_____

_____

_____

_____

_____

The Sun
WDYS

TODAY, I SAW THE sun shining. The sun is so bright and happy; it is simply lovely. It brings light and warmth to the earth even in the cooler seasons. The sun affects our moods in a positive way; it brightens my mood every day. There is less depression and sadness when the sun is shining.

However, there are also places that block the sunshine. Tall buildings and trees can provide welcome shade on the hottest of days. The sun is an essential part of life that we all enjoy.

Jesus asked me about the Son (Jesus) in my life. Where does He shine the most in me? Where is it easy for Him to shine? And where is it difficult for Him to shine? Are there things in my life that block Him from shining through me—for example, engaging in too much screen time, watching Netflix, or using other phone apps? What about the times when frustrations get the best of me? Is anger present and not controlled?

Yes, things, even good things, can block what the Son wants to do in our lives if we are not aware. When I give Him focus as I read the Word, His Son truly does shine through me.

John 8:12 ESV

Again Jesus spoke to them, saying, "I am the light of the world. Whoever follows me will not walk in darkness, but will have the light of life."

Is God the light of your life? Does His light shine in and through you every day? What are the things in your life that bring you His light and what are the things that block His light? WDYS?

_____

_____

_____

_____

_____

_____

_____

_____

_____

_____

_____

_____

_____

_____

_____

_____

_____

DAY THREE

Snow
WDYS

TODAY, AS I LOOK outside, I see snow. Last night while I slept, snow quietly blanketed our yard. Snow does not pick and choose what it covers. It is consistent, and as it falls, it covers all things in its path. Snow is white and gives an appearance of purity. It covers the mud, brown grass, driveways, parking lots, and the dreariness of winter. It brings with it beauty and the reminder that God still has the seasons in His hands.

So it is with the Holy Spirit. When He comes to us, we are covered by Him. He fills us with His presence and the understanding of God's Word as we read it. As we pray, He leads us in the direction and the decisions we need to make. He doesn't just cover us like a blanket of snow covers the ground. He is in us and a part of us, and He renews our thinking and brings us into the beautiful presence of God. He is more beautiful than the snow because His presence leads us in our understanding and deepens our walk with Jesus.

So today I pray, Holy Spirit, come live in me, draw me to God, and lead me in all my paths and decisions on this day. Cover me, fill me, draw me, speak to me. I am here, Lord; I am listening.

1 Corinthians 3:16 NKJV
Do you not know that you are the temple
of God and that the Spirit of God dwells in
you?

The Bible teaches that the Holy Spirit dwells within His people. He leads us by the hand and shows us the way we should go. Does He dwell within you? Where are you longing to be led by Him? WDYS?

_____

_____

_____

_____

_____

_____

_____

_____

_____

_____

_____

_____

_____

_____

_____

_____

_____

DAY FOUR

Leaves
WDYS

LOOKING OUT MY WINDOW today, I hear Jesus whisper "WDYS?" Snow has covered everything except a few leaves clinging to a tree. Through the rain, wind, snow, cold and harsh conditions, I can still see those leaves clinging to the branches of that tree.

I can see myself like one of those leaves. Like most people, I have experienced some difficult times over the years. Some of them include sicknesses, surgeries, loss of jobs, and overwhelming debt. I have lost family members through death and some friends who simply walked out of my life. I have experienced hurts and disappointments.

I am sure you have experienced similar times in your life. I know I am not unique. But, *only* God has been faithful through all these experiences and brought me through all my storms because I have learned to cling to Him.

Just as Jesus clung to a tree because He knew that His sacrifice would save the world, I trust in Jesus and cling tightly to Him through the storms of my life. I trust Him because of all that He has taught and revealed to me. Like a leaf clinging to the tree, I cling to the truth of the Word of God because He is my everything.

Deuteronomy 13:4 NLT
Serve only the LORD your God and fear
Him alone. Obey his commands, listen to
his voice, and cling to him.

Are you clinging to the one who loves you most today or are you letting the pressures of life pull you away from Him? There is no one whom you can trust more throughout your storms. Talk to Him about it. WDYS?

_____

_____

_____

_____

_____

_____

_____

_____

_____

_____

_____

_____

_____

_____

_____

_____

_____

_____

DAY FIVE

Bright Lights

WDYS

THE SUN IS SHINING on the neighbor's metal garage across the street from my house. The reflection on the metal is so bright that it hurts my eyes to look at it for very long.

In Exodus when Moses came down from the mountain with the Ten Commandments, his face shone. Scripture says ..."*Moses did not know that the skin of his face shone because he had been talking with God.*" Moses had to wear a veil so that the people would not be afraid of him.

You can tell when people have been in the presence of Jesus. They look different. They talk differently. They have different attitudes about things. The light of Jesus changes them.

Oh, how I want to shine for Jesus. I want to reflect what He is doing in my life. I want others to see what He is like by seeing the difference He makes in my life. When we allow the light of Jesus to reflect in and on us, we look and act differently. We carry His light to all whom we come in contact with.

2 Corinthians 4:6 NLT

For God, who said, "Let there be light in the darkness," has made this light shine in our hearts so we could know the glory of God that is seen in the face of Jesus Christ.

Jesus created you to know Him, so His light can shine through you. How do you describe light that looks like Jesus? What does it look like in a friend's life? In your life? WDYS?

_____

_____

_____

_____

_____

_____

_____

_____

_____

_____

_____

_____

_____

_____

_____

_____

_____

_____

DAY SIX

Clouds
WDYS

Today, I see the sun peeking through the clouds. It is beautiful to see that stream of light shining through the gray snow clouds.

I appreciate this because I live in the North where we see very little sunshine during the winter months. A lack of sunshine causes us to feel dreary, sullen, depressed, and gloomy. When we have a day of sunlight, our temperaments improve and we feel better about life. We smile more, and people smile back at us. We complain less about the weather and other things.

The scriptures teach us that God is light and that He gives us His light not only during the gray days of life but every day. His light shows us the way. It is what encourages us and shows us what we should do. It gives us peace and makes us feel alive. His light is found through the scriptures, in worshiping Him, and in spending time with other believers.

When His light shines on our path, we can see more clearly and follow Him more closely.

Thank you, Father, for Your light in my life.

John 8:12 NLT
Jesus spoke to the people once more and said,
"I am the light of the world. If you follow me,
you won't have to walk in darkness, because
you will have the light that leads to life."

What do you do on your gloomy days? Jesus says to follow Him and walk in His light. Do you have His light shining within you? What is Jesus showing you today about His light?

_____

_____

_____

_____

_____

_____

_____

_____

_____

_____

_____

_____

_____

_____

_____

_____

DAY SEVEN

Diamonds in the Snow
WDYS

TODAY IS A SUNNY winter morning, and as I look outside, I see the snow sparkling as though it was covered in diamonds. The sun shining on the snow is beautiful as it glitters, inviting thoughts of how much God loves to brighten our world with such a magnificent display.

As I think about diamonds in the snow, I am reminded of when my children were young and played in the snow. They loved to bundle up to go sledding and throw snowballs at each other. Eventually, the play would give way to the cold, bringing red cheeks and shivers followed by hot chocolate and warm blankets to warm up with.

God gives us diamonds much more valuable than the ones we wear on our fingers. My diamonds were my babies and were my most precious gifts. They were gifts from God and the sparkle they brought to my life made this momma very grateful and blessed.

As I have grown in the Lord, I have learned that walking with Him every day gives me a feeling that everything is well with my soul. Even when the days are hard and tiring, there is a peace and contentment that comes with just knowing your life is full of sparkly gifts that He has sent your way.

He is the One who fills our lives with special gifts that cause our hearts to sparkle!

Psalm 16:11 NKJV
You will show me the path of life;

In Your presence is fullness of joy;
At your right hand are pleasures forevermore.

Where in your life has God given you diamonds—special gifts just from Him? What gifts from Him are shining in your life today? Take a moment and thank Him for what He has shown you. WDYS?

_____

_____

_____

_____

_____

_____

_____

_____

_____

_____

_____

_____

_____

_____

_____

_____

Created to Remain
WDYS

I HEAR A WHISPER—"WDYS?" Today is very windy. The leaves once attached to the tree in my front yard are blowing around in the wind. Those leaves have let go of the tree and are now without a foundation or anything to hold on to. They are blowing aimlessly around and will most likely end up in a pile to be burned.

Things can happen in our lives that seem so overwhelming that it feels like we don't have the strength to hold onto God any longer. Satan, who is the enemy of our soul, is just waiting for an incident to occur in our lives that will cause us to let go of our faith and to stop believing the truth. He wants us to abandon what we believe, causing us to turn away from God.

If we let go of the truth of the Word of God and start to go in our own direction, we become vulnerable to being blown from one mistake to another without any purpose or hope. John 15 teaches that Jesus is the vine and we are the branches. If we separate ourselves from the vine, we no longer have the nourishment needed to grow and bear fruit.

When we refuse to let go and we stay connected to the vine, we have life. We can stay connected to Jesus, the vinedresser, through prayer, godly friends, worship, and church attendance. When things get tough, don't let go and risk being blown away. Rather, run to Him. It is never more important to be connected to the vine than when life is hard.

John 15:5–6 NLT
⁵ Yes, I am the vine; you are the branches.

Those who remain in me, and I in them, will produce much fruit. For apart from me you can do nothing.

[6] Anyone who does not remain in me is thrown away like a useless branch and withers. Such branches are gathered into a pile to be burned.

Are there any areas of your life where you are overwhelmed with the difficulties of life? Don't let go! Stay connected to the one true Vine. God is your personal vinedresser, caring and protecting every part of your life. WDYS?

_____

_____

_____

_____

_____

_____

_____

_____

_____

_____

_____

_____

Seasons

WDYS

Today, after a nudge from Jesus, I look outside and see the beautiful colors of fall. As the seasons change, I am reminded of the faithfulness of God in my life. He has designed our seasons. Both the seasons and God are loyal. They are consistent, expected, dependable, and trustworthy. They never change.

As God is in the seasons, so He is in us. He is consistent, expected, dependable, loyal, trustworthy, and always the same. His very nature is to be this way. He never changes.

We can trust God to always be the same. We are the ones who change. We are influenced by culture, other people, fads, styles, politics, and more to our own detriment. When we put our trust in Him, learn the scriptures, and apply them to our lives, we begin the journey of knowing Him and His faithfulness.

As the snow covers the ground in the winter, the trees change their colors in the fall, the flowers bloom in the spring, and the sun warms our land in the summer, we can put our trust in a God who is faithful and true to His Word and His ways. He is always the same!!

Hebrews 13:8 KJV
Jesus Christ the same yesterday, and today,
and for ever.

My favorite season is fall. I particularly love the colors in the trees, especially the red. It's as though God dumped buckets of paint in the trees. I love the cool days and digging out my warm jackets. What season do you love? Do you find the seasons to be dependable? Remember, Jesus is more dependable than the seasons He created. We can always trust that He will remain the same! WDYS?

_____

_____

_____

_____

_____

_____

_____

_____

_____

_____

_____

_____

_____

_____

_____

_____

_____

DAY TEN

A Fence
WDYS

Today, as I look out my window, I again hear the question in my ear, "What do you see today?" My response is, I see my neighbor's white picket fence in the front of their house.

Jesus asks me, "What are fences for?"

I respond that their purpose is to block off an area from people or animals. There are fences for protection from dangerous terrain. Parents put up fences to protect their children from getting hurt. Some are used to divide yards, and some are just for decoration. Some people paint them, and others hang flowers, plants, or decor on them.

I then hear Jesus say: "Are there fences in your life that keep you from Me?"

My immediate response is yes, rejection. I lived with that emotion early in my life, and it plagued me well into my adult years. Whenever I feel the fiery dart of rejection, I am taken back to those feelings I had as a little girl who experienced rejection regularly.

When I sinned or made a mistake, I was afraid that God would leave me and reject me because I had done something wrong. God does not leave us when we make a mistake. He loves us and protects us even when we sin. He reassures us and tells us to breathe and focus on Him. He will never reject us. All we must do is repent and be forgiven. He will still be there!

Like a fence protects a child from wandering off into dangerous territory, Jesus protects our hearts from the attacks of the enemy, keeping us safe in Him.

Hebrews 13:5(b) NKJV

"...I will never leave you nor forsake you."

Have you ever felt abandoned? Does that memory haunt you and make you feel that you are unloved? Remember God has promised to never leave us. He loves us more than we can even comprehend. What is He showing you today? WDYS.

_____

_____

_____

_____

_____

_____

_____

_____

_____

_____

_____

_____

_____

_____

_____

Spring Buds on the Tree
WDYS

TODAY, I AM SHOWN the spring buds on the maple tree, signifying new life. These tiny little buds hold the promise that they will mature into fully developed leaves. The skies are blue with white fluffy clouds, and a gentle breeze is blowing.

The breeze reminds me of the Holy Spirit. The Holy Spirit is gentle and leads me into the presence of Jesus. He shows me the direction I am to go when my thoughts are a little off-kilter. He shows me when I need forgiveness and how much I am loved by the Father.

I am so grateful for the gifts from the Father. I have asked myself where I would be without the Holy Spirit guiding my life. He reminds me that I am not alone and I am being cared for every minute of the day by my heavenly Father. As He guides me into a closer walk with Him, new buds grow within me that He will help mature, giving me new insights to Jesus that I can share with others.

Do you have the reassurance that you are loved by Jesus and that He is with you every day guiding your steps and leading you in the path you should follow?

Galatians 5:16 NLT
So I say, let the Holy Spirit guide your lives.
Then you won't be doing what your sinful
nature craves.

Do you feel that you are tossed around in your spiritual walk? Ask the Holy Spirit to guide your life. That is why He was sent. Ask Him to put your feet on a straight path and lead your daily steps. WDYS?

_____

_____

_____

_____

_____

_____

_____

_____

_____

_____

_____

_____

_____

_____

_____

_____

_____

_____

The Unforgiving Clock

WDYS

TODAY, AS I SIT at my desk to read the Bible and pray, I glance at the clock which reads 8:24 a.m. Unfortunately, this means I don't have the time to do my devotions today because I have to get ready for work. This frustrates me because I want to read and pray.

I realize I must prioritize my time with Jesus. Today, I ran out of time to spend with Him. While the clock is a good thing and reminds me of my obligations, it is also a reminder that our time is precious and not to be taken lightly.

Our walk with the Lord must be a priority. Being intentional about setting time aside to be with Him is important. He can't be our last-minute thought. Rather, He is to be our first thought in everything we do. Putting Him first sets up our priorities and makes everything else run smoothly.

I love how Jesus can use everything in our lives to remind us of Him, even the unrelenting clock! Thank you for the reminder, Father. I want You to be first in my life, and I want to be ready to do Your will every day.

Ephesians 5:15–17 NKJV

¹⁵ See then that you walk circumspectly, not as fools but as wise, ¹⁶ redeeming the time, because the days are evil.

¹⁷ Therefore do not be unwise, but understand what the will of the Lord is.

Do you let time slip away from you? Are you so busy that you don't spend time with Jesus every day? The only way to build a relationship with our Father is to spend time with Him. Is He speaking to you about time management? Take a moment and listen to Him speaking to your heart. WDYS?

_____

_____

_____

_____

_____

_____

_____

_____

_____

_____

_____

_____

_____

_____

_____

_____

_____

DAY THIRTEEN

Dark Clouds
WDYS

AGAIN TODAY, I HEAR Him asking, WDYS? Have you ever noticed how dark the clouds become when a storm is on its way but the sun is shining in part of the sky? Those clouds seem so much darker in contrast to the brightness of the sunny sky. Today, the sky is partially dark and partially sunny, reminding me of how life can be. Some days are sunny and bright, and others are cloudy and dark.

As believers, we have the Son of God with us all the time, bringing light into the cloudy or dark places of our lives. When things seem the darkest, Jesus is there to shed light into the darkness and help us see clearly. He is the one who brings light into our days and nights!

We must also remember that we will have dark days. There is no promise that when we know Jesus our life will always be sunny. Our faith is tested and proven during the trials of life. Learning to lean into Him and trust Him during those dark times is how we grow and mature in Him.

I really like sunny days, but I understand that if I am to grow and mature in Him, I must have cloudy days too.

John 8:12 NIV

When Jesus spoke again to the people, he said, "I am the light of the world. Whoever follows me will never walk in darkness, but will have the light of life."

Are you in a dark place right now and can't seem to find your way out? Jesus is there, just waiting for you to ask Him for help. He is the light we need in all our days. Ask Him to help. What is He saying to your heart today? WDYS?

_____

_____

_____

_____

_____

_____

_____

_____

_____

_____

_____

_____

_____

_____

_____

_____

_____

DAY FOURTEEN

The Flag Waving in the Wind
WDYS

Today, Jesus showed me the flag waving in the wind. The American flag is the symbol of our freedom and the symbol of the land in which we live. The flag is respected and honors every state within our country. Our cherished freedom is something that Americans have fought and died for.

Some people believe that serving God sets boundaries too high and keeps them from having fun. They enjoy their lifestyle and don't want to change. They think that believers are boring and can't participate in life. Some just have a hard time understanding and are happy the way they are.

What they do not understand is the freedom we have in Jesus. Knowing Him gives us the strength not to be addicted to drugs, alcohol, sex, power, and all the vices clamoring for our attention. As believers, we have the power of God in our lives to live in freedom, away from the bondage of sin that destroys those who are caught up in sin.

Are we free from troubles? Absolutely not. However, when there is trouble, we have a source to help us beyond our expectations and to give us a full, satisfying life.

Ephesians 3:20–21 NKJV

[20] Now to Him who is able to do exceedingly
abundantly above all that we ask or think,
according to the power that works in us, [21] to
Him be glory in the church by Christ Jesus
to all generations, forever and ever. Amen.

Do you live in freedom, or is your life full of bondage to things or people? As a follower of Jesus, you will find freedom! What is He showing you today about freedom? WDYS?

_____

_____

_____

_____

_____

_____

_____

_____

_____

_____

_____

_____

_____

_____

_____

_____

_____

DAY FIFTEEN

Rainbows

WDYS

As I sit down today, I am drawn to the sun shining on my diamond engagement ring and making beautiful colorful rainbow reflections on my desk and walls. He says, WDYS?

Have you ever known someone who is beautifully radiant? It is as though they have rainbows shining from their eyes. They have a beautiful smile, and their disposition is gentle, kind, peaceful, and loving. They appear to be happy in their own skin. They beam from the inside out, and you feel special in their presence. These are the kind of people I enjoy being around.

The presence of God looks the same way in our lives. We are filled with beautiful words, kindness, goodness, self-control, love, and all those fruits mentioned in Galatians 5. The fruits we grow from knowing Jesus is what will make us have a beautiful disposition because we are becoming like Him.

When we know Jesus and want to share Him with others, we will show them the love, joy, peace, and kindness that comes from within us. This is Jesus living within our hearts and His love being poured out to others. Scripture teaches us that we will be known by our fruits. We can show people God in our lives just by allowing Him to live through us. Our lives will be full of color as we live in Him.

Galatians 5:22–23 NKJV

22 But the fruit of the Spirit is love, joy, peace, longsuffering, kindness, goodness, faithfulness, 23 gentleness, self-control. Against such there is no law.

What does your life reflect? Which fruit do you desire to have shining out of you today? As we submit to Him, His fruit will grow in us. WDYS?

_____

_____

_____

_____

_____

_____

_____

_____

_____

_____

_____

_____

_____

_____

_____

_____

_____

_____

DAY SIXTEEN

Books

WDYS

Today, as God asks "What do you see" and I look around, I am shown my bookcase. Many books rest on those shelves. Some I have read, and some I have not. I have many from when I studied for my credentials and degree, and some books are self-help. Some stories are about people, some devotionals, some Bible studies, but most importantly, there are Bibles. I have multiple translations of the Bible for better understanding of the Word.

You might ask why? Because the Bible was authored by God. Within it is all the information necessary to know God and live as He wants us to. Not only that, but when we ask the Holy Spirit, He will give us understanding of what we are reading as well.

I once saw a pastor open the Bible and hold it out before us. He said if we could see with spiritual eyes, we could actually see it moving up and down as though it were breathing. Why? Because the Bible is alive and breathes on us as we read it. It is God's Word and is life-changing. He brings life and understanding of who He is through the Word.

Books are great; I love them. But, unlike books, the Word of God is inspired by God and is a living book. God actually breathes on us and changes us one day at a time, and as we apply it to our lives, He helps us become who He has called us to be—the children of God.

Joshua 1:8 ESV

This Book of the Law shall not depart from
your mouth, but you shall meditate on it

day and night, so that you may be careful
to do according to all that is written in it.
For then you will make your way prosperous,
and then you will have good success.

Is the Bible an important part of your life? Do you read it regularly? If you do, you will hear God speaking to you. If you don't, you won't. What is God saying to you today about His Word? WDYS?

_____

_____

_____

_____

_____

_____

_____

_____

_____

_____

_____

_____

_____

_____

DAY SEVENTEEN

The Sunrise
WDYS

TODAY, I SAW THE sunrise, and it brought light to the day. The day had started out quite dark. As the sun steadily climbed, the sky became brighter and brighter.

The Word of God tells me that God is light. In Him, there is no darkness. Absent from Him there is darkness, but not the kind of darkness we see at night when there are no lights. Rather, it is a darkness of our mind and soul and the inability to see rightly, because our mind is governed by the darkness of this world. The ruler of this world is Satan, and he brings darkness into the lives of those who don't know Jesus. The only way to have the light of Jesus in our life is to be in His Word and to know who He is.

As I spend time in His Word, His message becomes part of who I am. The darkness of misunderstandings and the lies that I have believed begin to fade. As I begin to fill myself with the light of His Word, I am then able to bring His light, or the understanding of who He is, to others. The light of God becomes more brilliant as I spend more time with Him. With each moment I spend in his presence, I receive more light of who He is. As He gives me understanding, I am able to be His light to those around me.

John 14:30 NLT
"I don't have much more time to talk to you,
because the ruler of this world approaches.
He has no power over me."

John 8:12 NIV

When Jesus spoke again to the people, he said, "I am the light of the world. Whoever follows me will never walk in darkness, but will have the light of life."

How do you bring Jesus's light to rule in your life when there is darkness, confusion, uncertainty, or fear? Turn to Him today. He will bring His light into your life. Can you hear Him speaking to you? WDYS?

_____

_____

_____

_____

_____

_____

_____

_____

_____

_____

_____

_____

_____

_____

_____

DAY EIGHTEEN

Pictures

WDYS

TODAY, I LOOKED DOWN at my desk and saw a picture of me holding my first newborn granddaughter outside in front of my sunflowers in my garden. I held her tightly as she was wrapped up in a warm blanket. The smile on my face was so huge, and I was very happy.

My first granddaughter is a teenager now, but the memory of that moment and the gift she was and still is to our family is as strong as that day in my backyard. The words to express how I felt are hard to articulate. The love that was building up inside of me just wanted to burst out of my body. When I held my other four grandchildren, I felt that same feeling—a realization of how blessed I was to be able to hold them and love them.

As I think about how much I love her, I am reminded of how much God loves us. He holds us tightly and wraps us in His love and cares for us just as we do for our babies in this life. God is life. He came that we would have life and live an abundant life. He loves you and me so much that He gave His life for us, and by knowing Him we might live with Him for all eternity.

John 15:13 KJV
Greater love hath no man than this, that a
man lay down his life for his friends.

There is no love like the love of Jesus. He bore unbearable pain and suffering on the cross so that we could know Him and spend eternity with Him. Do you love Him? Are you ready? WDYS?

Fallen Leaves

WDYS

LEAVES AREN'T MEANT TO hold fast to the tree limbs in autumn. The leaves were designed to let go and fall to the ground where they turn into dirt and fertilize the ground for the next generation of grass and trees. They have lived their life cycle, and then it is time for them to nurture the ground for the next season of life.

Our pastor has said on numerous occasions that once we are saved it is no longer about us. Our job is to share what we have received so that more people will come to know Jesus. We are actually meant to die to our wants and desires and allow Jesus to lead us where He wants us to go. We aren't meant to hold tightly to positions; we must loosen our grip and allow the next generation to learn after our cycle is complete. We are to empower them to become who we once were and even better. We must decrease to make room for the younger generation to increase so that they can lead the next generation. Our influence will remain through their leadership, and we will enjoy the fruit of our example by allowing them to lead throughout their lives.

Life is a cycle. It continues to move. We can't get comfortable where we are. We must be willing to listen to what God is speaking to our hearts and let go of what we are holding on to so that He can put something new into our hands. It can be scary because we like where we are. But when we trust Jesus, we know He has His best in store for us next and the new might just be better than the old.

¹⁹ "Go therefore and make disciples of all nations, baptizing them in the name of the Father and of the Son and of the Holy Spirit, ²⁰ teaching them to observe all that I have commanded you. And behold, I am with you always, to the end of the age."

We are instructed throughout scripture to teach the younger generation about Jesus and His kingdom. We must teach them how to live soberly and uprightly and serve Him every day. As we teach, we assure that His Word will go forward and not be forgotten. We live in a world full of people who do not love Jesus—either because they've never been taught or they refuse to accept His teachings.

Who is Jesus telling you to teach? Are you to instruct your children, grandchildren, coworkers, friends? Be obedient today and go and tell them about Him! WDYS?

_____

_____

_____

_____

_____

_____

_____

_____

_____

_____

DAY TWENTY

Blurry Vision
WDYS

TODAY, I AM HAVING a hard time seeing. A few weeks ago, I had eye surgery, and now my eyesight is blurry. My glasses are no longer able to correct my vision, and my eyes are still healing. It is frustrating! I bought cheap drug-store glasses, but they do not help. I must be patient and wait until my eyes are healed and then get my new prescription. As each day passes, I notice that I can gradually see a little more clearly.

Jesus spoke to my heart during this time and said that I would have times in my life when I would not be able to see with my eyes. At times, we can only see through faith. Other times, we can only rely on the Word that we have received as we go along our journey. Does that mean that we won't see with our eyes again? Not at all. Rather, it means that this is a time to trust in what I know, not what I see.

I have seen things with my eyes and not understood what I was looking at. People carry emotions, experiences, frustrations, and sadness that we cannot see. I want to be able to see with God's eyes. His eyes are never blurry. I don't want to depend on my own understanding. I want Him to give me understanding, insight, and discernment into what I am looking at because my eyes will fail me. Only His eyes can see clearly.

Proverbs 3:5–6 NLT
⁵ Trust in the LORD with all your heart; do
not depend on your own understanding.

^{6} Seek his will in all you do, and he will show
you which path to take.

We definitely will go through difficult times—times that scare us, make us cry, or bring confusion and a lack of understanding. These are NOT times to turn away from Jesus. Rather, those are times to draw closer than ever to Him. These are the times to seek Him and listen carefully to what He says. We can rest assured that His plans are always full of hope and not disaster!

If you are struggling today, draw close to Him and listen. Don't forget to write down what He shows you! WDYS?

_____

_____

_____

_____

_____

_____

_____

_____

_____

_____

_____

_____

_____

_____

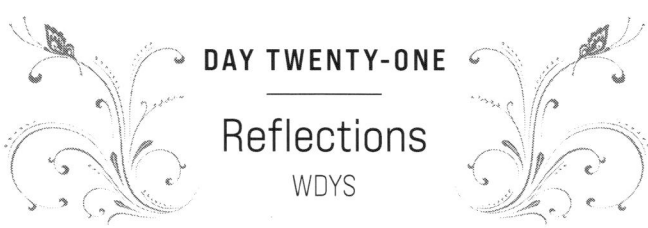

Reflections

WDYS

TODAY, I WAS PREPARING to go to church and team preach with a co-preacher from my church. I woke up early praying about the service and sharing the Word He had given me. I was concerned that what I had prepared was not what the Lord wanted me to share. As I looked out my window, I saw the reflection of an outside light on my neighbor's window. I didn't see the actual light, only a reflection of it. After seeing the reflection, the Lord spoke to my heart and said to me that I would be a reflection of Him today when I spoke. He told me not to be concerned about it because I had prepared and was ready.

As believers, we are His reflection everywhere we go, whether it's the office, the bank, or the grocery store. Everywhere we go, we are either reflecting Him in a positive or a negative way.

What an honor it was to share what Jesus had given me on that Sunday. No matter what your calling is in life, everywhere you go, you reflect who Jesus is in your life. Reflect Him well

2 Corinthians 3:18 ESV

And we all, with unveiled face, beholding the glory of the Lord, are being transformed into the same image from one degree of glory to another. For this comes from the Lord who is the Spirit.

As we walk with Jesus, read His Word, worship Him, and get to know Him more and more, we begin to reflect Him. We become like those we are around. If we are around those who do evil things, we will be like them. However, if we are around those who truly love Jesus and are trying to reflect Him, we'll become like Him. Who do you reflect in your life? WDYS?

_____

_____

_____

_____

_____

_____

_____

_____

_____

_____

_____

_____

_____

_____

_____

_____

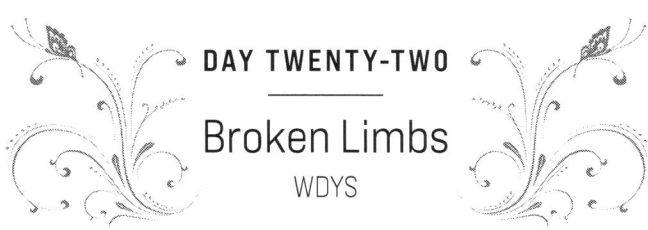

DAY TWENTY-TWO

Broken Limbs
WDYS

A VERY STRONG STORM with high winds passed through my neighborhood. As a result, some branches and small limbs were blown off my tree. As I looked out today, I saw the limbs on the ground, but I also saw that the tree was standing firm.

We all have storms in our lives that cause our hearts to hurt and cause us pain. It is not possible to have sunshine every day. Scripture tells us that there will be rain, there will be storms, and there will be trouble. What the scriptures also tell us is that, when we have storms, we are to *trust* in *Him* and we will remain standing.

Philippians 4:8–9 NIV

8 Finally, brothers and sisters, whatever is true, whatever is noble, whatever is right, whatever is pure, whatever is lovely, whatever is admirable—if anything is excellent or praiseworthy—think about such things.

9 Whatever you have learned or received or heard from me, or seen in me—put it into practice. And the God of peace will be with you.

If we focus on the storm and not on Jesus, we will be afraid. We must turn our thoughts to Him, and then we will have peace. What storm do you need Him to walk through with you today? WDYS?

_____

_____

_____

_____

_____

_____

_____

_____

_____

_____

_____

_____

_____

_____

_____

_____

_____

Cardinals

WDYS

TODAY, I SEE A male and female cardinal together eating seed from our feeder. I see God's design in them. The color of the female is much more muted compared to the bright red color of the male. They are paired together to propagate. Next summer, I will see more of them at my feeder.

The Lord showed me that cardinals were on the ark and have remained present since that time. They are not disturbed about world affairs, but rather they live their lives according to their design. They have no idea how much beauty they bring to nature. They only live as they were designed to live.

If that were only true for us humans. There is so much confusion about who we are and what our purpose is. The Bible is clear about who we are in Him; however, the enemy has perverted God's plan, and people have believed his lies. The only way to know our purpose is to know God. He shows us throughout the scriptures who He is and who we are.

We are His children. He loves us unconditionally. He wants to know us and us to know Him. He has set out a life plan for us, and it is our responsibility to find it. How do we find it? Through a relationship with Him.

Matthew 6:26 NLT

Look at the birds. They don't plant or harvest or store food in barns, for your heavenly Father feeds them. And aren't you far more valuable to him than they are?

We are much more valuable than the birds. He has made us just a little lower than the angels. One day, if we know Him, we will spend eternity with Him. Know who you are today. You are God's daughters and sons, and He loves you with an unfailing love. Do you need to know your purpose? Talk to Him about it. WDYS?

_____

_____

_____

_____

_____

_____

_____

_____

_____

_____

_____

_____

_____

_____

_____

_____

DAY TWENTY-FOUR

Dwelling Places
WDYS

TODAY, I SEE A small euonymus alatus or burning bush outside my window. It is bare of leaves because we are still in winter. In its branches is a small bird's nest which housed little birds last summer. I remember them flying out of the nest. Just as God created birds with the knowledge to build a house for their young, so He created us with the ability to build homes for our dwelling places.

Even more important than a physical home for us is understanding that, when we are believers, we are the dwelling place of the Holy Spirit. God actually dwells in us! We are His home on earth!

How do you know if God lives in you? It begins with believing that Jesus is the Son of God who died for your sins and accepting what scripture teaches about Him. After you accept Him, He then comes to live in you. You begin to seek Him, and you are changed. Your thoughts, your dreams, your plans all change because you are now forming a relationship with the God who created you. You have now become His dwelling place. As He lives in you, you will begin to live for Him.

1 Corinthians 3:16–17 NKJV

¹⁶ Do you not know that you are the temple of God and that the Spirit of God dwells in you?

¹⁷ If anyone defiles the temple of God, God

will destroy him. For the temple of God is holy, which temple you are.

1 Corinthians 6:19 NLT
Don't you realize that your body is the temple of the Holy Spirit, who lives in you and was given to you by God? You do not belong to yourself,

When we accept Jesus, the Holy Spirit comes to reside in us. We are no longer our own; we belong to Him. This makes us more aware of His presence in our lives. This causes us to hunger for Him and seek Him more. We have His presence with us every day, hour, and minute. Knowing this, how will you cultivate His presence in your daily life? Are you aware that He is there? WDYS?

_____

_____

_____

_____

_____

_____

_____

_____

_____

_____

God's Children
WDYS

TODAY, I SEE MY prayer list on my desk. I keep this list to help me remember to pray for people. This list includes the names of family members, friends, and others who I am aware of who need prayers. Some of them do not know Jesus. Some of them are sick and need healing. Some of them have asked for prayer. Others are having difficulties in their marriages. Some of them are walking close to Jesus and just want to know Him more. All of them need Jesus.

Have you ever had a name or seen a picture of someone you know just go across your mind? I have many times. When this happens, I always pause and pray for that person. God teaches us to pray for people, and I believe this is just one way He tells us to pray for that person.

We are all part of the family of God. We are all brothers and sisters and are responsible for one another. When one of us is hurting, we are all hurting. My goal is to be available to pray for anyone who has a need. Thus, the prayer list that reminds me to pray. You see, I am still human and given to forgetfulness at times. I am grateful for that reminder I see on my desk.

1 Timothy 2:1–4 NLT

¹ I urge you, first of all, to pray for all people. Ask God to help them; intercede on their behalf, and give thanks for them. ² Pray this way for kings and all who are in authority so that we can live peaceful and quiet lives

marked by godliness and dignity. [3] This is good and pleases God our Savior, [4] who wants everyone to be saved and to understand the truth.

We are to be people of prayer. Do you pray? As you can see, it pleases God when you do. Who needs your prayers today? What is God saying to you about praying for others? WDYS?

_____

_____

_____

_____

_____

_____

_____

_____

_____

_____

_____

_____

_____

_____

New Life

WDYS

Jesus is asking me today, "What do you see?" As I look outside, I see it is a cloudy, chilly morning. Despite the temperature, I see beautiful yellow flowers blooming. I always get so excited in the spring when flowers begin to poke up out of the ground. It is the promise of warmer weather. That means no boots, no coats, and no hats. It is joyful just to think about the warmth after a long, cold winter.

The significance of this scene is the new life we have in Jesus. It is like the freshness of the first warm day, the delicate nature of the flowers, and how beautifully and intricately they are designed. They energize me and excite me about the summer weather that will soon arrive.

We never know what a new day will bring, but every day with Jesus brings new life. However, Jesus always has us in His hands, and we can trust Him to bring about His will in our lives. It is exciting and glorious to be in the center of His will, waiting to see what He will do with us today. It is like the promise of springtime.

2 Corinthians 5:16–17 NLT

[16] So we have stopped evaluating others from a human point of view. At one time we thought of Christ merely from a human point of view. How differently we know him now!

[17] This means that anyone who belongs to Christ has become a new person. The old life is gone; a new life has begun!

New life as a believer is a spiritual life—a new way to think and act. New life is laying down our old ways and picking up His ways. It is learning about Jesus and living according to His Word. It does not mean we are perfect, only forgiven. Have you been given new life through Jesus? Does it excite you to see what He will do next through you? Talk to Jesus about it. WDYS?

_____

_____

_____

_____

_____

_____

_____

_____

_____

_____

_____

_____

_____

DAY TWENTY-SEVEN

Back Home
WDYS

TODAY, JESUS SAYS, "LOOK outside. WDYS?" Our neighbors, who winter in Florida, came home. Their house sits empty of activity throughout the winter months. My husband and I walk through their house from time to time just to check on it and so it does not appear empty and abandoned. What a joy it brings to my heart to see them home and see life again in that house!

Rejoicing over our neighbor's arrival made me think of how Jesus must feel when someone returns to Him after they've experimented with the world and discovered that they need Him. What joy He must feel to see life return to the one who was lost when they choose Him over the world.

The enemy wants us to believe that we are missing something if we believe and put our faith in Jesus. Scriptures teach us that Satan is the father of lies. As such, he convinces people to believe those lies. He entices them to participate in behavior that does not line up with God's plan for their lives. He leads them astray into pain and brokenness and away from Jesus who loves them. Jesus says in John 10:10 that the thief, or enemy, comes to steal, kill, and destroy, but Jesus came to give us an abundant life.

If you have been drawn back into the world, now is the time to come back home. Maybe you know someone who has walked away from Jesus. There is joy unspeakable waiting for them and you in the arms of Jesus, our Father. Come home.

John 10:10 NKJV

The thief does not come except to steal, and

to kill, and to destroy. I have come that they may have life, and that they may have it more abundantly.

Can you hear Him calling you? You may not need to be called to come home, rather just to come to Him. In any case, He is waiting for you to call out to Him. WDYS?

_____

_____

_____

_____

_____

_____

_____

_____

_____

_____

_____

_____

_____

_____

_____

_____

Our Second Home

WDYS

Friends of ours have a beautiful camper. This camper is nicer than our home. It has slide outs, a laundry area, a kitchen, a large bed, and a shower. It has everything one needs to live quite comfortably. Our friends live in this "camper" in the winter, and it becomes their second home.

Jesus said He had nowhere to lay His head or a place to call home when He walked on the earth. This was by His choice. He doesn't mean He doesn't want us to have a place to lay our heads. In fact, He delights in giving His children gifts.

Jesus's work on earth is done. He has returned to His home in heaven, which is described as being indescribable! Currently, He resides in each one of us who have received Him as our Savior. His spirit is in me and in you.

We also have a second home that is being prepared for us. This home will be more beautiful than words can describe because God is the architect of that home. One day my home will not be on earth any longer. The best thing about our new home is we will live in the presence of Jesus for all eternity. All sickness, sin, and evil will be gone from our lives forever.

1 Corinthians 2:9 NKJV

But as it is written:
"Eye has not seen, nor ear heard,
Nor have entered into the heart of man
The things which God has prepared for
those who love Him."

Do you have confidence that you will be with Jesus when you leave this world? If you have accepted Him, believe the Word that teaches us who He is, and have a relationship with Him, you are guaranteed to see Him one day and live with Him forever. If you have never accepted Him, don't wait a second longer, now is the time. If you have, I'll meet you in heaven one day, and together we will worship our Lord and Savior. Take a moment and talk with Him about eternity. WDYS?

_____

_____

_____

_____

_____

_____

_____

_____

_____

_____

_____

_____

_____

_____

_____

_____

DAY TWENTY-NINE

Rain Drops

WDYS

TODAY, RAIN IS STARTING to fall. I can see the leaves on the burning bushes outside my window bouncing back after each drop hits them. Rain is so important to the life of our plants, and, even though they are being pounded by water, it is as if they know they will survive and be stronger after the rain has passed.

As believers, rain comes into our lives too. Some is light rain that we can handle with no problems. Other times, a fierce storm tries to take us out. Whether the rain is light or a fierce storm, our Savior is there with us giving us the strength and victory over the storm.

We do not ever walk alone when we know Jesus. We always have Him at our side. He is just waiting for us to believe that our prayers will be answered and to ask Him for help.

Psalm 27:4–6 NLT

⁴ The one thing I ask of the LORD—
the thing I seek most—
is to live in the house of the LORD all the
days of my life,
delighting in the Lord's perfections
and meditating in his Temple.

⁵ For he will conceal me there when troubles
come;

he will hide me in his sanctuary.
He will place me out of reach on a high rock.

⁶ Then I will hold my head high
above my enemies who surround me.
At his sanctuary I will offer sacrifices with shouts of joy,
singing and praising the LORD with music.

Are you in the rain today? Allow it to accomplish the goal for which it was sent. If you don't know, ask God. He will show you. Remember, He stands next to you and within you, and He is waiting to hear from you. Write down what He tells you today. WDYS?

_____

_____

_____

_____

_____

_____

_____

_____

_____

_____

_____

_____

DAY THIRTY

Stuck

WDYS

TODAY, AS I SIT down and look out my window, He says, "What do you see?" I look and see a bug stuck in a spider web. The bug is not getting out of the web unless it is removed. It can twist and turn, but the web is too sticky and will hold him tightly there.

I am reminded that we must be diligent as believers not to believe the lies of the enemy. He will tell us lies or the partial truth to confuse us and to keep us from knowing the truth that saves us. If we are caught in his web, getting out can be difficult. It can take time and bring consequences in our lives.

We can't always depend on our own thinking. We must depend on God's thinking to keep us safe. Webs are spun every day to try to trap us. When we stay alert, stay in the Word, stay in worship, and spend time with Him, He will show us and we will be aware and know the dangers ahead of us.

Genesis 4:7 NLT

You will be accepted if you do what is right.
But if you refuse to do what is right, then
watch out! Sin is crouching at the door, eager
to control you. But you must subdue it and
be its master.

I don't believe that sin is just outside our door waiting to jump on us. It can be a series of mistakes, or even a calculated plan, that causes us to get trapped in sin. The way to not get caught in the web is to stay connected to Jesus. The Holy Spirit is the one who will guide and direct us, when we ask Him and stay connected with Him. Are you caught today? All is not lost. Repent, turn around, and go the other way. Jesus is waiting for you to cry out. Write down what He tells you. Are you doing well today? Keep it up. Someone out there may be relying on your strength. WDYS?

_____

_____

_____

_____

_____

_____

_____

_____

_____

_____

_____

_____

_____

_____

_____

_____

Color vs. Black

WDYS

TODAY IS FULL OF color. All around, I see vibrant flowers of many different colors. I see birds flying around, and again, so much color. The sun shining on creation magnifies the color that is on the earth. I love the summer because of how beautiful it is, and it always brings my thoughts to God and his awesome creation.

In contrast to beautiful color is the color black. Black is a color that results from absorption of all visible light. If there is no light, we are in darkness. The enemy brings darkness because he has no light in him. His only goal is to destroy the faith of believers and take them away from God.

The Bible encourages us to live in the light of God where there is no darkness and where one can see. I can't see when the lights go out at night. It takes a few minutes for my eyes to adjust. I want to be able to see color and Jesus every day of my life and keep darkness far away.

Acts 26:15–18 NLT

¹⁵ "Who are you, lord" I asked.

And the Lord replied, "I am Jesus, the one you are persecuting. ¹⁶ Now get to your feet! For I have appeared to you to appoint you as my servant and witness. Tell people that you have seen me, and tell them what I will show you in the future. ¹⁷ And I will rescue you from both your own people and the Gentiles. Yes, I am sending you to the Gentiles [18] to open their eyes, so they may turn from darkness to light and from the power of Satan to God. Then they will receive forgiveness for their sins and be given a place among God's people, who are set apart by faith in me."

This passage is when God called Paul into ministry. God told Paul what he was to do. As you can see, darkness is an absence from God and light is in God's presence. Where are you today? Are you walking in darkness or in the light? Jesus is calling you today too, just like Paul. Come out of the darkness and walk with Him in the light. WDYS?

_____

_____

_____

_____

_____

_____

_____

_____

_____

_____

_____

Dew on the Grass

WDYS

THERE ARE WHISPERS IN my ear, WDYS? Today, I see dew on the grass. Dew is little droplets of water sprinkled across the earth. The dew covers the grass and stays until the heat of the day burns it away.

Water cleanses, refreshes, and cools down the heat of the previous day. Water brings freshness to the morning and liquid for bugs, birds, and worms. The morning dew replenishes, nourishes, and cleans the air bringing refreshment to the earth. The dust from the previous day settles, and a new day begins.

When we start our days with Jesus, we receive that same replenishment, nourishment, and cleansing. His presence focuses us on the new day and renews our minds and thoughts. His mercies are new every morning. Being in His presence I receive Him, hear Him, draw close to Him, and am refreshed by being in His presence.

Coming to spend time with Jesus is just as refreshing to us as the dew is refreshing to the land. Being in His presence refreshes my soul.

Lamentations 3:22–23 ESV

22 The steadfast love of the LORD never
ceases, his mercies never come to an end;
23 they are new every morning;
great is your faithfulness.

Each morning is a new day to come to Jesus. We leave the past behind us and embark on a new day. On that day, the expected and unexpected will happen. We can be sure that He will be with us throughout this day. He is faithful to keep His Word.

Talk to Him early in the morning and ask Him to be with you throughout your day. WDYS?

_____

_____

_____

_____

_____

_____

_____

_____

_____

_____

_____

_____

_____

_____

_____

_____

_____

DAY THIRTY-THREE

Walls
WDYS

I CAN EVEN SEE Jesus in the walls. Okay, I can hear you saying *what*? Well, think about it. We have plaster, metal, brick, wood, aluminum, vinyl, drywall and many other materials used in buildings. How can I see Jesus in the walls? Is His image stamped in the building materials? Of course not.

The scripture I used on the Foundation page teaches that He is in everything and everything is in Him. He didn't actually make the walls. However, He gifted us with creative abilities by teaching us to use the natural resources, gifts, and abilities He gave us to design and produce many things that we use daily. We can see the same with cars, planes, trains, roads, clothing, medicine, money, textiles, etc. All these things were made possible because He created and gave us the resources to make them.

Nothing is new to Him. He knows all things, sees all things, and is in all things. Yes, I see Him in all the good things I am blessed to experience, but Jesus saw them first!

John 1:3 NIV
Through him all things were made; without
him nothing was made that has been made.

Have your eyes been opened to see Him in all things yet? Ask Him to show you and reveal Himself to you even in everyday things. He wants you to know Him in all things. He will hear you and show you things you can't imagine. WDYS?

Seeing Jesus in the Scriptures

THE FIRST HALF OF this devotional journal was meant to open our eyes to seeing Jesus everywhere in everyday life. I have always seen Him in nature. The stories I shared were a few of the daily encounters I experienced while on this journey. They show Him as caring, exact, detailed, dependable, perfect, loving, steadfast, committed, and reliable. The list goes on and on.

Jesus can be counted upon in our daily lives to be true to His nature and to fulfill all the promises that are in His Word. He will always be who He says He is. He cannot be anyone else. Never has there been another person who is totally sinless and who has our best interests as His main priority. The only thing Jesus wants from us is that we believe who He is, thereby cultivating a relationship with Him and telling others about Him. In doing so, we spread His Word and give others the opportunity to know and experience Him in their lives.

The second half of this book focuses on seeing Jesus in the scriptures. Since He *is* the scriptures, that is not hard to do. You will see His character and how He has shown Himself to me through the Bible. The passages I share are ones that have been very dear and special to me during my walk with Jesus. They have formed me, matured me, nurtured me, and reminded me of who my Father really is and how much He loves me. They are not meant to create a deep theological discussion, rather they are subjective in how they are applicable in your daily walk with Him.

The little things in life are so important. Those fifteen, twenty, and sixty minutes you spend daily reading, praying, and growing in Him make such a difference in your life. These are the times I want to share with you. I am not anyone special. I only want to share with you what the Father has shared with me. I am just someone who wants to know Jesus more and more each day. As I have grown to know Him more, I want to know Him even more.

Please continue to journal as He shows you Himself in your daily time with Him. Open your heart to understand how greatly you are loved and learn how to love Him back. The time you spend with Him is priceless and life-altering, lifegiving, and lifesaving.

DAY THIRTY-FOUR

Water or Wine?

John 2

WDYS in the Scriptures

JESUS TURNED WATER INTO wine in John 2 when He attended a wedding. This story is the first reported miracle of Jesus. The story goes that they ran out of wine and Jesus's mother came to Jesus asking Him to do something about the situation. Jesus told her that it was not His time yet, but He still performed the miracle by having the purification water pots filled with water and then turning that water into wine. When the wine was served, the host (wedding coordinator) exclaimed to the groom how good the wine was and that he was surprised the groom had saved the best wine for the end of the festivities. (Everything Jesus does is the best).

This story bothered me a little. There seemed to be deception in the story because Jesus allowed the people to believe that the groom had saved the best for last, but knowing in my heart that Jesus cannot be deceptive because His nature is only good all the time, *I dug a little deeper*. Miracles are performed in our lives every day that we are unaware of. Traffic accidents averted, illnesses healed, marriages saved, and people's lives changed because of the power of the Holy Spirit.

In this particular miracle, the only people who knew the water was turned to wine was Jesus's mother, the servants, and any disciple who was with Jesus at the time. This miracle, being His first miracle, was meant to help His friends and was not meant as a lesson for the attendees. However, as is always true for everything Jesus did, the miracle had a deeper meaning.

Jesus is the one who transforms us. Knowing Him is a miracle every day because the sin nature we are born with is transformed into a loving, kind, and spiritual nature which changes who we are. It may not seem like a miracle, but if we were left with our sin nature and never had the opportunity to know God, we would be headed for eternal death and separation from Him.

Just as Jesus turned the water into wine, He changes our stony hearts into pliable hearts that can receive Him and be transformed by His love. He cares more about us than we care about ourselves.

John 2:4 NKJV
Jesus said to her, "Woman, what does your concern have to do with Me? My hour has not yet come."

You see, Jesus is concerned with what we are concerned with. He knows all about us and acts endlessly on our behalf. What do you need from Jesus today? What is He speaking to your heart right now? Make a note of it here. WDYS?

_____

_____

_____

_____

_____

_____

_____

_____

He Sees You

Psalm 139 NKJV

WDYS in the Scriptures

God's Perfect Knowledge of Man

¹ O Lord, You have searched me and known me.
² You know my sitting down and my rising up;
You understand my thought afar off.
³ You comprehend my path and my lying down,
And are acquainted with all my ways.
⁴ For there is not a word on my tongue,
But behold, O LORD, You know it altogether.
⁵ You have hedged me behind and before,
And laid Your hand upon me.
⁶ Such knowledge is too wonderful for me;
It is high, I cannot attain it.

⁷ Where can I go from Your Spirit?
Or where can I flee from Your presence?
⁸ If I ascend into heaven, You are there;
If I make my bed in hell, behold, You are there.
⁹ If I take the wings of the morning,
And dwell in the uttermost parts of the sea,
¹⁰ Even there Your hand shall lead me,
And Your right hand shall hold me.

¹¹ If I say, "Surely the darkness shall fall on me,"
Even the night shall be light about me;
¹² Indeed, the darkness shall not hide from You,
But the night shines as the day;
The darkness and the light are both alike to You.

¹³ For You formed my inward parts;
You covered me in my mother's womb.
¹⁴ I will praise You, for I am fearfully and wonderfully made;
Marvelous are Your works,
And that my soul knows very well.
¹⁵ My frame was not hidden from You,
When I was made in secret,
And skillfully wrought in the lowest parts of the earth.
¹⁶ Your eyes saw my substance, being yet unformed.
And in Your book they all were written,
The days fashioned for me,
When as yet there were none of them.

¹⁷ How precious also are Your thoughts to me, O God!
How great is the sum of them!
¹⁸ If I should count them, they would be more in number than the sand;
When I awake, I am still with You.

¹⁹ Oh, that You would slay the wicked, O God!
Depart from me, therefore, you bloodthirsty men.
²⁰ For they speak against You wickedly;
Your enemies take Your name in vain.
²¹ Do I not hate them, O Lord, who hate You?
And do I not loathe those who rise up against You?
²² I hate them with perfect hatred;
I count them my enemies.

²³ Search me, O God, and know my heart;
Try me, and know my anxieties;
²⁴ And see if there is any wicked way in me,
And lead me in the way everlasting.

I had to share this entire chapter with you. This chapter, in my opinion, is who Jesus is and why I love Him so much.

As a child, I was not raised by my parents. I was in a home similar to a foster home. I spent my earliest years believing that no one loved me and that I was a mistake. My mother was off doing her own thing and only had what I refer to as "paper children," our yearly school pictures which she passed around to her extended family. However, she never really knew us because we only saw her a few times a year.

All of that being said, this chapter shows me who I really am. I am loved so much that He knows when I stand up and when I sit down. He knows every thought I have, even before I have them. There is nowhere I can go to get away from Him, because He is everywhere.

He knows everything I do, think, and say before I do it. In fact, He knew me before I was born. He knew me while I was being formed in my mother's womb. He knew all the days that I would live and everything that I would ever do. He even knew that I would be sitting at my computer typing this now.

My favorite verses in this chapter are verses 13–18.

¹³ For You formed my inward parts;
You covered me in my mother's womb.
¹⁴ I will praise You, for I am fearfully and wonderfully made;
Marvelous are Your works,
And that my soul knows very well.
¹⁵ My frame was not hidden from You,
When I was made in secret,
And skillfully wrought in the lowest parts of the earth.
¹⁶ Your eyes saw my substance, being yet unformed.

And in Your book they all were written,
The days fashioned for me,
When as yet there were none of them.

[17] How precious also are Your thoughts to me, O God!
How great is the sum of them!
[18] If I should count them, they would be more in number
than the sand;
When I awake, I am still with You.

Why am I not a mistake? Because He made me. He has a plan and a purpose for my life not only here on this earth, but also for eternity.

Every word I just spoke about me is also true for you. You are fearfully and wonderfully made. He knows you, He sees you, He loves you, and He wants to be with you.

If you doubt this deep within your heart, please read this chapter again. Once you've digested it, consider how important and dearly loved you are by Him.

If you already know the love of Jesus, affirm with Him how much you love Him and how important He is in your life. What is Jesus saying to you right now? What is He showing you? Write it down. WDYS?

_____

_____

_____

_____

_____

_____

_____

_____

He Draws You

John 6
WDYS in the Scriptures

ONE SUNDAY AS I was preparing to pray before services, God showed me a big red and gray magnet at the auditorium entrance. Do you remember those big red magnets shaped like a horseshoe and had silver on the tips? That is what I saw at the doorway into the church. God spoke to my heart saying that as we prayed and people entered the worship service, the junk, the cares, concerns, pains, and difficulties would be drawn off them by this magnet. (Of course, God is the magnet). Having their burdens drawn away would free them from the distractions of life and allow them to enter into worship and be open to the Word.

While my vision was a beautiful picture of how much God wants our hearts and minds free of distraction, I understood that God draws us to Himself, as a magnet draws metal to itself. He wants us to come to Him, no matter where we are or what we have done.

No one can know Jesus unless they are drawn to Him by God. If you know Jesus, you are already aware that He is constantly drawing you to Himself.

John 6:44 NIV
No one can come to me unless the Father
who sent me draws them, and I will raise
them up at the last day.

Have you felt that tug at your heart telling you to get out of bed and go to church? Or maybe that tug is calling you to your quiet place to read, pray, and spend time with Jesus. This is Jesus drawing you. He is asking you to come and be with Him and to set time aside time to listen to Him. He wants us to make Him more important than anything else in our lives. Is He drawing you today? WDYS?

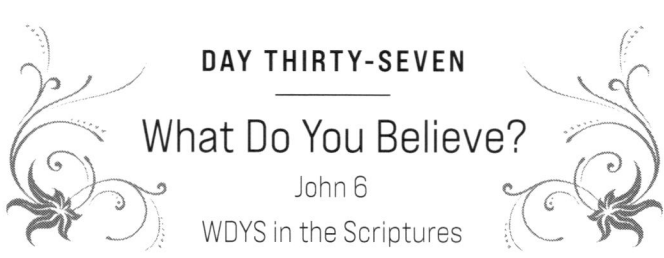

DAY THIRTY-SEVEN

What Do You Believe?

John 6

WDYS in the Scriptures

WHILE I WAS IN the hospital a couple years ago, I was reading scripture and came upon a verse in John 6. Jesus had performed many miracles, and people around Him had witnessed these miracles. He had just fed the multitude of people with only a few fish and bread, and the people were intrigued with Him. They didn't understand who He was or how He had performed those miracles. They just wanted to be able to do what He did.

In verse 28, the people asked Him how they could do the work that He had done. Jesus, knowing that their hearts still didn't understand Him, said to them: "This is the only work God wants from you: Believe in the one he has sent" (John 6:29 NLT).

Recently, I have had my own struggle with belief as my husband is undergoing medical tests that could result in a quite serious diagnosis. But throughout this ordeal, I have believed in the healing power of Jesus. This morning, I woke up praying that God would heal my husband and asking for strength to walk through this trial. I asked God to help me with the fear I had been dealing with. I told Him I didn't want to fear, but I was struggling with it. Shortly after praying, I looked at my phone and saw a text from a friend. She had sent me a picture of a plaque I had given her. On the plaque was simply the word *Believe*. I was immediately reminded that belief, trust, and confidence in God is what dispelled fear in my life. I believe God sent me that word through my friend!

While I'm writing this, I still don't know what the outcome of the tests will be, but I do know that all I need to do is believe. I have trust in Him that He is who He says He is and that He has this situation in His hands. I am believing that my husband is healed, yes, in Jesus's name I believe.

John 6:29 NLT

Jesus answered and said to them, "This is the only work God wants from you: Believe in the one he has sent."

My question to you today is do you believe? Have you learned to believe and trust God in those dark, difficult times? Even as believers, we are still human beings and can have moments of fear, doubt, and unbelief. When that happens, allow God to remind you that all He wants is for us to believe and trust in Him. The rest is in His hands. WDYS?

_____

_____

_____

_____

_____

_____

_____

_____

_____

_____

_____

Firewood

John 1

WDYS in the Scriptures

In Genesis 22, we find the story of Abraham and Isaac. Isaac is the child for whom Abraham and Sarah waited for many years. One day, God tells Abraham to take Isaac and sacrifice him on the altar.

Immediately, Abraham obeys. My mind would have been doing flip-flops and trying to figure out a way to change God's mind or even bargaining with Him. Not Abraham. God said it; Abraham did it. Abraham takes with him all the necessary items for a sacrifice, such as wood, and starting a fire, etc.

Isaac is asked to carry the wood for the fire, and up the hill they go. Abraham proceeds with the task at hand and lays Isaac on the altar and raises his knife. Immediately, he is stopped, and a ram is provided for the sacrifice.

I believe Abraham was such a man of faith that he knew God would either raise Isaac from the dead or provide another sacrifice.

We see two pictures in this story. Isaac is a picture of Jesus who willingly laid down his life, and the wood Isaac carried is a picture of the cross on which Jesus was crucified. Isaac was spared, and a ram was provided.

Jesus was our sacrificial lamb on the altar. We all deserve to be on the altar, but Jesus went in our place. He was the one who took our sins and provided us a life with Him forever.

John 1:29 NKJV

The next day John saw Jesus coming toward
him, and said, "Behold! The Lamb of God
who takes away the sin of the world!"

I wrote this book for only one reason—to share with you how Jesus reveals Himself every day. If you do not know Him, there is no time like today to stop what you are doing and turn your heart over to Him. Simply pray, tell Jesus you believe, and ask Him to come into your heart. He will come to you immediately. Next, please find a church who preaches Jesus's love and start your journey of seeing God every day.

If He has spoken to your heart, please write down your experience with Him here. WDYS?

Names

Revelation 21
WDYS in the Scriptures

TODAY, I WANT TO be transparent and honest. As I was reading Nehemiah 3, I was a bit bored. Name after name, family after family, and in all honesty, I will never remember all those names. So why? Why did God include all the names of the people who helped Nehemiah rebuild the walls of Jerusalem? I asked Him.

God is so specific and detailed. In the first section of this book, we learned how detailed God was in creation. He is also detailed in what He does and how He does it.

In Nehemiah 3, God journals the process of rebuilding the walls. No one is left out. Every detail is included in this journal. Did He do this because He didn't want to forget? Or maybe because He wanted us to know who worked on the wall? No, I don't think so. He did it because He *sees* us. He knows everything we do. We are very important to God, and *nothing* goes unnoticed.

He knows what our gifts are, and He puts us in the proper place to use them for His glory. Your Name is important to Him. Your gifts are important to Him. You have them to bless Him and others. Do you use your talents to the glory of God? Do you give Him back what He has given you?

The Bible is still being written—are there chapters where your name is written down?

Revelation 21:22–27 NLT

²² I saw no temple in the city, for the Lord God Almighty and the Lamb are its temple.

²³ And the city has no need of sun or moon, for the glory of God illuminates the city, and the Lamb is its light.

²⁴ The nations will walk in its light, and the kings of the world will enter the city in all their glory.

²⁵ Its gates will never be closed at the end of day because there is no night there.

²⁶ And all the nations will bring their glory and honor into the city.

²⁷ Nothing evil will be allowed to enter, nor anyone who practices shameful idolatry and dishonesty—but only those whose names are written in the Lamb's Book of Life.

This passage is about heaven, and look, there is a book with your name written down—if you've received Him as your Savior. Is your name in the book? WDYS?

_____

_____

_____

_____

_____

_____

DAY FORTY

Jesus Prays for ME
John 17
WDYS in the Scriptures

JOHN 17 IS ONE of my favorite chapters in the Bible. In this chapter, Jesus is hours away from the cross and is praying to His Father. He knows what is about to happen. He goes to the garden and pours His heart out to His Father, God. He talks about His authority to give eternal life to all who know Him. He explains that eternal life is knowing God and Jesus Christ. Then He tells His Father that He has completed the work He had been sent to do and that they both share in the glory of pleasing the Father. He prays for His disciples and tells His Father that they belong to Him. He says that He is not praying for the world, rather He is praying for His disciples.

A disciple is a learner who is under discipline from their teacher. Everyone who believes in Jesus is *His* disciple. That means that if you believe and live for Jesus, you are counted as a disciple. A disciple believes what the teacher is teaching and submits themselves to the teaching. Jesus asks God to keep the disciples safe from the evil one as they are sent out into the world to bring His message.

In verse 30, He prays for all those who will believe in Him in the future! He prays that they would be in Him and He will be in them. In other words, they accept His teaching and make it their life's work to follow Him. This prayer Jesus prayed was for you and me. He prayed for us before He willingly went to the cross to give His life for you and for me. He prayed for our protection and unity and that the evil one (Satan) could not have us.

He gives them His glory so that they will be united. When we know Jesus, we also know God because Jesus is God.

John 17 NLT

1 After saying all these things, Jesus looked up to heaven and said, "Father, the hour has come. Glorify your Son so he can give glory back to you. 2 For you have given him authority over everyone. He gives eternal life to each one you have given him. 3 And this is the way to have eternal life—to know you, the only true God, and Jesus Christ, the one you sent to earth. 4 I brought glory to you here on earth by completing the work you gave me to do. 5 Now, Father, bring me into the glory we shared before the world began.

6 "I have revealed you to the ones you gave me from this world. They were always yours. You gave them to me, and they have kept your word. 7 Now they know that everything I have is a gift from you, 8 for I have passed on to them the message you gave me. They accepted it and know that I came from you, and they believe you sent me.

9 "My prayer is not for the world, but for those you have given me, because they belong to you. 10 All who are mine belong to you, and you have given them to me, so they bring me glory. 11 Now I am departing from the world; they are staying in this world, but I am coming to you. Holy Father, you have given me your name; now protect them by the power of your name so

that they will be united just as we are. [12] During my time here, I protected them by the power of the name you gave me. I guarded them so that not one was lost, except the one headed for destruction, as the scriptures foretold.

[13] "Now I am coming to you. I told them many things while I was with them in this world so they would be filled with my joy. [14] I have given them your word. And the world hates them because they do not belong to the world, just as I do not belong to the world. [15] I'm not asking you to take them out of the world, but to keep them safe from the evil one. [16] They do not belong to this world any more than I do. [17] Make them holy by your truth; teach them your word, which is truth. [18] Just as you sent me into the world, I am sending them into the world. [19] And I give myself as a holy sacrifice for them so they can be made holy by your truth.

[20] "I am praying not only for these disciples but also for all who will ever believe in me through their message. [21] I pray that they will all be one, just as you and I are one—as you are in me, Father, and I am in you. And may they be in us so that the world will believe you sent me. [22] "I have given them the glory you gave me, so they may be one as we are one. [23] I am in them and you are in me. May they experience such perfect unity that the world will know that you sent me and that you love them as much as you love me. [24] Father, I want these whom you

have given me to be with me where I am. Then they can see all the glory you gave me because you loved me even before the world began! ²⁵ O righteous Father, the world doesn't know you, but I do; and these disciples know you sent me. ²⁶ I have revealed you to them, and I will continue to do so. Then your love for me will be in them, and I will be in them."

I love this passage of scripture. To me, it shows how much Jesus loves us. His prayer to His Father, at a time of great anxiety and self-sacrifice, was not about Him, but rather about you and me. He was sealing in His heart that all who follow Him would be safe through Him and securing the promise for us that we will live eternally because of His sacrifice. When I pray, I want to be that determined for my family, friends, fellow believers, unsaved, and the world. What does this prayer of Jesus mean to you? How do you feel after reading it? How does your heart feel? WDYS?

_____

_____

_____

_____

_____

_____

_____

_____

_____

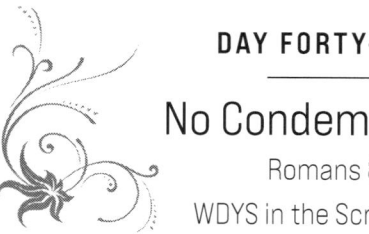

No Condemnation

Romans 8

WDYS in the Scriptures

WHEN I WAS A child, I was not raised by my parents. My mother gave me to a woman who raised children for income. My mother periodically sent money to this woman for keeping me and my sister. This arrangement was sort of like a foster home but with no state involvement. It was simply an agreement between two people. When my mother failed to send the money, which she did on a regular basis, life became hard. My "foster" home then became a difficult place to live, and my "foster" mother could be a taskmaster, insistent that we earn our keep one way or another. As a child I didn't understand why my life was so different from my friend's lives.

I started attending a little church in our neighborhood, and for the first time in my life I felt love from others. That love I felt was the love of Jesus, although at such a young age I didn't totally understand it. Even to this day, many years later, I struggle with the true meaning of love.

From my childhood perspective, to be accepted and "loved" meant that you had to perform and do things. "Love" was accompanied by requirements and tasks. As I began to know Jesus more and more, I began to understand that His love has no conditions and that His love is there just because I exist. I didn't have to do anything to earn His love. I only needed to believe in Him.

My life changed so much after I came to know Jesus. I felt so different inside. My home was still the same, but the difference was that Jesus was now with me and He carried me through many hard times and still does to this day. Knowing Jesus is what life is all about.

Romans 8:1 always takes me back to my childhood. I think it was one of the first verses I memorized. At home I was constantly condemned for not doing what I was supposed to do or not doing it in a manner that pleased them. In this little church, full of people who just loved me, I learned that the love of Jesus has nothing attached to it and that there wasn't any condemnation in Him. All I had to do was believe in Him. His love isn't based on my being good or doing things perfectly. Rather, He loves me because I am His daughter and He is always good. He pours His love and goodness into me every day.

Romans 8:1 NKJV

There is therefore now no condemnation to those who are in Christ Jesus, who do not walk according to the flesh, but according to the Spirit.

How about you? Do you feel unloved and condemned? If you don't know Jesus, He is standing in front of you right now just waiting for you to accept Him and believe in Him. All you have to do is say YES to Him. Open your heart and let Him in. Tell Him that you believe and you want Him to come into your life and change you. This begins a journey of walking with the Creator of the universe. He knows you, loves you, and has no condemnation for you because you will be in Christ Jesus! If you know Jesus, you are not condemned!!! What is He showing you today? WDYS?

_____

_____

_____

_____

Martha, Martha

Luke 10
WDYS in the Scriptures

HAVE YOU EVER WONDERED why you are the only person working while everyone else is sitting around talking and eating? Or have you prepared a large meal and afterward everyone goes in the other room and leaves you with the cleanup? I have been in that situation which frustrates me at times. I must also admit, I am a recovering perfectionist! Things always need to be done a certain way for me to be content. However, I am learning to relax, enjoy my family and friends, and just go with the flow. The work will always be there, but the relationships being nurtured are more important than the work needing done.

Today, I want to look at the story of Martha and Mary in Luke. Jesus went to their house to visit. Martha was busy cooking, cleaning, and preparing for her guests. When Jesus arrived, Mary, her sister, sat down at Jesus's feet and listened to all He had to say. They were all friends, so I imagine their conversation was about the groups he had sent out to prepare His way in the next towns and about the parable he had told about the man who had been beaten and left on the roadside. Jesus always taught his disciples and followers, and Mary wanted to hear all about it.

Martha discovers Mary just sitting there and says to Jesus, "Hey, what about me? Do I have to do all the work while Mary just sits here?" The thing I love about this story is that Jesus is so patient. He gently explains to Martha that Mary is doing nothing wrong and that she was fine listening to what He had to say. He didn't scold Martha for wanting help, rather He told her that some things are more important than others and that Mary sitting at His feet was more important for her than helping with the meal.

Sometimes, we get our priorities all messed up. Jesus's message to Martha is that we need to put first things first. He is first. The meal can wait. The cleaning can wait. The phone can wait. The TV show can wait. Have we spent time with Him today is the question. Do we put Him first? He wasn't upset that Martha was cooking; the question was her priority. What was she putting first?

Luke 10:38–41 NKJV

38 Now it happened as they went that He entered a certain village; and a certain woman named Martha welcomed Him into her house. 39 And she had a sister called Mary, who also sat at Jesus' feet and heard His word. 40 But Martha was distracted with much serving, and she approached Him and said, "Lord, do You not care that my sister has left me to serve alone? Therefore tell her to help me."

41 And Jesus answered and said to her, "Martha, Martha, you are worried and troubled about many things. 42 But one thing is needed, and Mary has chosen that good part, which will not be taken away from her."

When we consider our own lives, we must always remember to put Him first. Nothing is more important than our relationship with Jesus. He gives all of us twenty-four hours in a day and the freedom to choose what to do with it. Let's remember that our relationship with Jesus must come first, and then everything else will flow into place perfectly! What is Jesus showing you today about spending time with Him? WDYS?

Friends with Faith

Mark 2

WDYS in the Scriptures

THE STORY IN MARK 2 highlights the impact of our faith for others. Scholars believe that during this story Jesus is at Peter's house, which is packed with people inside and out. There was no room to squeeze in even one more person. By this time, the news of Jesus had spread, and people were coming from all around to see and hear Him speak.

As the story opens, a group of four men are carrying a paralyzed man on a mat. They desire for Jesus to heal their friend. When they discovered that they cannot get in the house to see Jesus, they carry their friend to the roof of the house, begin tearing off the roof, and lower him to Jesus. Of course, this causes quite a stir and gets Jesus's attention. Jesus has a conversation with the paralyzed man, and the man believes in Jesus and is healed.

I totally love all the stories of Jesus healing, but this story strikes my heart because that man wouldn't have been with Jesus if his friends hadn't brought him. They not only brought him to Jesus, but they also had amazing faith—to the degree that they did whatever they needed to do to get their friend to Jesus.

Mark 2:1–12 NLT

¹ When Jesus returned to Capernaum several days later, the news spread quickly that he was back home. ² Soon the house where he was staying was so packed with visitors that

there was no more room, even outside the door. While he was preaching God's word to them, ³ four men arrived carrying a paralyzed man on a mat. ⁴ They couldn't bring him to Jesus because of the crowd, so they dug a hole through the roof above his head. Then they lowered the man on his mat, right down in front of Jesus. ⁵ Seeing their faith, Jesus said to the paralyzed man, "My child, your sins are forgiven."

⁶ But some of the teachers of religious law who were sitting there thought to themselves, ⁷ "What is he saying? This is blasphemy! Only God can forgive sins!"

⁸ Jesus knew immediately what they were thinking, so he asked them, "Why do you question this in your hearts? ⁹ Is it easier to say to the paralyzed man 'Your sins are forgiven,' or 'Stand up, pick up your mat, and walk'? ¹⁰ So I will prove to you that the Son of Man has the authority on earth to forgive sins." Then Jesus turned to the paralyzed man and said, ¹¹ "Stand up, pick up your mat, and go home!"

¹² And the man jumped up, grabbed his mat, and walked out through the stunned onlookers. They were all amazed and praised God, exclaiming, "We've never seen anything like this before!"

Do you need to take an inventory of who your friends are and their influence in your life? If you were sick, would they pray with faith and believe for your healing? Would they call you, pray for you, bring you food, and come and take care of you? What about you? What kind of friend are you? Do you pray when someone asks you to and do you believe for their healing or whatever their need might be? I want friends like the four in this story. What is Jesus saying to you? WDYS?

_____

_____

_____

_____

_____

_____

_____

_____

_____

_____

_____

_____

_____

_____

_____

_____

_____

DAY FORTY-FOUR

Peter Restored

Luke 22
WDYS in the Scriptures

IN LUKE 22, WHEN Jesus had his last supper with the disciples just prior to His crucifixion, he had a conversation with Peter. In verses 31–34 Peter states that he would go to prison and even die with Jesus. Jesus responds to Peter and predicts that Peter will deny Him three times during that night before the rooster crowed in the morning. In fact, Peter did deny Jesus three times. In verse 61, after he denied knowing Jesus the third time, Jesus turned and looked at Peter. Peter remembered what Jesus predicted, and he left the courtyard and wept bitterly.

The good news is that this story doesn't end here. In John 21 after Jesus was crucified, Peter, John, and some of the other disciples went fishing. When they looked toward the shore, they saw a man who looked like Jesus. After recognizing that it was Jesus, Peter leaped out of the boat and went to see Him. Jesus had prepared breakfast for them, and they all sat down and spoke with Him. Jesus began another conversation with Peter in which He asked him three times if he loved Him. Frustrated, Peter answered yes to each inquiry of Jesus. Afterward, Jesus told Peter about how he would give his life to serving Him. Jesus was restoring Peter, establishing that Peter did love Him, and making sure that Peter realized it as well.

John 21:15–19 NLT

15 After breakfast Jesus asked Simon Peter, "Simon son of John, do you love me more than these?"

"Yes, Lord," Peter replied, "you know I love you."

"Then feed my lambs," Jesus told him.

[16] Jesus repeated the question: "Simon son of John, do you love me?"

"Yes, Lord," Peter said, "you know I love you."

"Then take care of my sheep," Jesus said.

[17] A third time he asked him, "Simon son of John, do you love me?"

Peter was hurt that Jesus asked the question a third time. He said, "Lord, you know everything. You know that I love you."

Jesus said, "Then feed my sheep.

[18] "I tell you the truth, when you were young, you were able to do as you liked; you dressed yourself and went wherever you wanted to go. But when you are old, you will stretch out your hands, and others will dress you and take you where you don't want to go."

[19] Jesus said this to let him know by what kind of death he would glorify God. Then Jesus told him, "Follow me."

This story could be about any of us. We all sin and deny Jesus by the way we live our lives. The good news is that when we repent (turn from our sin and go back to Jesus) we are forgiven. Just as Peter was forgiven for his sin and restored to a right relationship with Jesus, so are we.

I love how Peter was not afraid to run to Jesus when he realized He was there. When we make mistakes or sin, we should not run from Jesus, rather we should run to Him because He is always there. He is the one who lovingly restores and puts us back into the right relationship with Him.

Perhaps you are saying "Oh, not me. I have sinned too big for God to forgive me." Not true. God is standing ready to forgive all sins. The Bible teaches us that whoever calls on the name of the Lord will be saved, and if we confess our sins, He will forgive us. None of us are worthy, but all of us qualify for forgiveness. What is Jesus saying to your heart right now? What is He showing you? Pray and receive your restoration, then write it down. WDYS?

_____

_____

_____

_____

_____

_____

_____

_____

_____

_____

_____

_____

_____

_____

DAY FORTY-FIVE

Our Plans

Jeremiah 29:11

WDYS in the Scriptures

WHEN I WAS A young girl, I used to think of God as a huge figure up in the sky who had a big stick and was ready to beat me whenever I made a mistake. I was afraid of Him and, at that time, I didn't understand that God loved me and that He had a plan for my life.

As I matured in my walk with the Lord, I learned about Jeremiah 29:11 which teaches that God didn't just drop us on the planet and walk away. He has a plan for each of us. That plan is a good plan, full of hope and promise.

Even though He has a plan for us, we can rebel against His plan and do things our way, but that wouldn't be the best option for us. When we submit, fully surrender to Him, and give Him our lives, He will then lead and guide us into His perfect plan for our lives.

> Jeremiah 29:11 NIV
>
> "For I know the plans I have for you," declares the LORD, "plans to prosper you and not to harm you, plans to give you a hope and a future."

Recently, I have been trying to decide about making a change in my life. I don't want to make this change, but I know it is the right decision to make. My problem is trusting that, after the change is made, God will bring me to a new place even better than where I am now. When we trust

God and obey His promptings, we can believe that He has something even better for us because His plans are to give us a future and a hope. I believe He will, do you? What is God saying to you? WDYS?

_____

_____

_____

_____

_____

_____

_____

_____

_____

_____

_____

_____

_____

_____

_____

_____

_____

_____

Seek and Live

Matthew 6

WDYS in the Scriptures

ARE YOU A WORRIER? At times I allow the circumstances in my life to cause me to worry. In the Sermon on the Mount, Jesus simply says do not worry about everyday life. He even lists some of the things we tend to worry about—food, drink, clothes, money. I could add to that list, but you already know what you worry about. Jesus continues by comparing us to birds who are tiny little creatures and are fed daily. But I love what He says next—they are fed by the heavenly Father! God feeds them!

God loves all of His creation—birds, flowers, and US! As He takes care of the birds and the flowers, He will take care of us. Later in Matthew 6, He says that worry dominates the thoughts of unbelievers, but worry should not dominate the thoughts of a believer. God knows our needs, and He *will* take care of us. Rather than worry about things, we are to seek His face, seek His heart, seek His kingdom, seek *Him* and live a righteous life. When we do this, all these things we worry about will be provided!

Matthew 6:28–34 NLT

28 "And why worry about your clothing? Look at the lilies of the field and how they grow. They don't work or make their clothing, 29 yet Solomon in all his glory was not dressed as beautifully as they are. 30 And if God cares so wonderfully for wildflowers

that are here today and thrown into the fire tomorrow, he will certainly care for you. Why do you have so little faith?

[31] "So don't worry about these things, saying, 'What will we eat? What will we drink? What will we wear?' [32] These things dominate the thoughts of unbelievers, but your heavenly Father already knows all your needs. [33] Seek the Kingdom of God above all else, and live righteously, and he will give you everything you need.

[34] "So don't worry about tomorrow, for tomorrow will bring its own worries. Today's trouble is enough for today."

We all have concerns and worry from time to time. When those times come, go to the Father who feeds the birds. He will take care of whatever your need is. What is He saying to you today? Write it down.

_____

_____

_____

_____

_____

_____

_____

_____

DAY FORTY-SEVEN

Curly Hair

Luke 12
WDYS in the Scriptures

I HAD A PASTOR who said that to question God is to find fault with Him. Ouch, that hurts because there are times when I wish my appearance were different. I have very thick, coarse, curly hair that is oftentimes unmanageable. Over the years I have yearned for a smooth, flowing head of hair. You ask, what is the point of this? Good question.

God cares so much about us that He even knows how many hairs are on our heads. To me that is just amazing, because I know there are tons on my head! But way more important than that is the degree in which we are loved. Jesus speaks about the sparrows and their value being very little monetarily, yet He does not forget a single one of them. How much more He loves you and me! If He loves a sparrow, and I am sure there are millions of them, and never forgets one of them, imagine how He loves and cares about you and me. We are created in His image, in the image of God! *He loves you*!!! You are His sons and daughters. He desires you more than you can ever imagine.

Luke 12:6–7 NLT

⁶ "What is the price of five sparrows—two copper coins? Yet God does not forget a single one of them. ⁷ And the very hairs on your head are all numbered. So don't be afraid; you are more valuable to God than a whole flock of sparrows."

DAY FORTY-SEVEN · 107

Do you believe that God loves you? Is it sealed in your heart, or do you constantly remind yourself of how bad you are and that God could never love you? If this is the case, please talk to God about it. Jesus wants us to believe His Word, not the lies that unbelief brings to our minds. *Believe* what the Word of God tells us. You are precious in His sight, and you are loved. He loved *you* so much that He died for you. What is He saying to you right now? WDYS?

Greater Is HE

1 John & 2 Corinthians

WDYS in the Scriptures

HAVE YOU EVER THOUGHT "This is just too hard. I can't do this anymore. I am tired, weak, and I quit!" Have you concluded that people are nuts and you just can't handle it anymore? I think if you are really honest with yourself, you will agree that there have been moments like that. The frustrations of everyday life can sometimes become overwhelming.

When I have felt like quitting, the Lord always reminds me that I am not doing life in my own strength. In 2 Corinthians 12 it says that we are made perfect in weakness. When we are weak and we let go of trying to do it ourselves, we allow God to lead us. We cannot walk the Christian life on our own. We were not meant to. Rather, we are to depend daily on Him, sometimes hourly and even every minute.

In John 4 we read that He is the greater one within us. Our power is not our own. Our power, strength, determination, and victory all come from God. Anytime we succeed, He gets the glory. Anything good in my life is because of *Him*.

I was right. I cannot do this on my own. It is the strength of Jesus who gets me through my days, my hard places, my misunderstandings, my carelessness, and my inabilities. It is only through Him that I can face each day.

1 John 4:4 NKJV

You are of God, little children, and have

overcome them, because He who is in you is greater than he who is in the world.

2 Corinthians 12:9–11 NKJV

[9] And He said to me, "My grace is sufficient for you, for My strength is made perfect in weakness." Therefore most gladly I will rather boast in my infirmities, that the power of Christ may rest upon me. [10] Therefore I take pleasure in infirmities, in reproaches, in needs, in persecutions, in distresses, for Christ's sake. For when I am weak, then I am strong.

What do you do when you realize you can't handle things on your own? Do you give up? Rather than admitting defeat, rely on God to get you through your difficulties. He is ready and waiting for you to come to Him. What is He saying to you today? WDYS?

_____

_____

_____

_____

_____

_____

_____

_____

DAY FORTY-NINE

Not Good Enough
Romans 3
WDYS in the Scriptures

A FEW YEARS AGO, I was involved in a mentoring program with our pastoral team from church. A dear couple who had been pastors for many years led the group. We were all gathered together in their living room discussing our walk with the Lord. I said to the group that at times I just didn't feel good enough. One of the leaders looked me in the eye and said, "That's because you're not good enough." Wow, that set me back for a moment until I thought it through. He was absolutely right. I am not good enough. Isaiah says that our righteousness is like filthy rags to God. Nothing we do could ever earn a place with Him or measure up to His greatness.

Romans 3 discusses that the law couldn't save men because they could not keep the law. Their works didn't save them. And, we have all sinned and fallen short of the glory of God. None of us, not even one, is worthy of Jesus. It goes on to say that our righteousness comes from the redemption that is in Jesus! We are saved not because of what we have done but because of what HE did for us.

My pastor friend was right. I am not good enough and will never be good enough in my own strength. It is only through the redemption of Jesus that I will stand before Jesus. He is good enough!!!

Romans 3:19–26 NLT (underline added)

¹⁹ Obviously, the law applies to those to whom
it was given, for its purpose is to keep people

from having excuses, and to show that the entire world is guilty before God. ²⁰ For no one can ever be made right with God by doing what the law commands. The law simply shows us how sinful we are.

²¹ But now God has shown us a way to be made right with him without keeping the requirements of the law, as was promised in the writings of Moses and the prophets long ago. ²² <u>We are made right with God by placing our faith in Jesus Christ.</u> And this is true for everyone who believes, no matter who we are.

²³ For everyone has sinned; we all fall short of God's glorious standard. ²⁴ Yet God, in his grace, freely makes us right in his sight. He did this through Christ Jesus when he freed us from the penalty for our sins. ²⁵ For God presented Jesus as the sacrifice for sin. People are made right with God when they believe that Jesus sacrificed his life, shedding his blood.

Are you trying to live the Christian life in your own strength? If you are, you are not good enough! Put all your strength in Him, trust Him, surrender your walk to Him, and allow Him to lead you. What is He saying to you today about your walk with Him? WDYS?

DAY FIFTY

Why Pray?

1 Thessalonians 5
WDYS in the Scriptures

PAUL GAVE SOME INSTRUCTIONS to the Thessalonians in Thessalonians 5. In verse 17, he instructs the Thessalonians to pray without ceasing. That instruction may seem hard to accomplish if we don't understand the meaning of what Paul was teaching. If we take the instruction literally, we are to spend all our waking hours in prayer. While that would be a wonderful thing to do, it would be impossible because of obvious reasons.

Rather than praying every minute of our day, we are to have a heart for prayer. A consistency in prayer allows us to be a breath away from prayer at all times. There are times when sirens are blaring, the weather is causing terrible conditions for people, or people are caught in earthquakes and fires. There are times when our finances are exhausted. And times when we pray for those who simply need Jesus. There are countless needs that should be taken to God in prayer every day.

The scriptures even teach that we are to pray for those who despitefully use us or who are unkind to us. In other words, we are to live in a constant mind frame that would lead us to pray at a moment's notice for whatever circumstances are currently occurring in our lives.

Prayer is part of a relationship with Jesus. It is communicating with Him regularly, telling Him about our life, and believing in His intervention on a daily basis. While we are grateful for our food, it is not only praying grace over our meals and a quick prayer at night.

Because I sometimes forget to pray for others, I discovered a good practice for me is to keep a prayer list with the people and things I pray for on a regular basis. We can keep the list in our Bible, in our phones, or on the office desk. Keep the list in front of you at all times because it helps remind us to pray and to constantly be bringing people before the Lord in prayer.

When someone I know crosses my mind, I pray for them. As a believer we are called to a life of prayer. As people who pray, we will be praying for everyone we know at one time or another because we all face times when prayer is important and necessary in our lives. The reverse is also true. As God sends faces and names to us to pray for, He also sends our face or name to those who will lift us up in prayer when we have no idea it is even happening.

1 Thessalonians 5:16–18 NKJV

[16] Rejoice always, [17] pray without ceasing, [18] in everything give thanks; for this is the will of God in Christ Jesus for you.

Prayer is not some super religious thing that we do. It is simply communicating with Jesus about our lives, friends, needs, and circumstances. Prayer is asking for His intervention in all those things while believing His intentions are always good for His people. Do you pray? Do you believe God hears and answers your prayers? What is He saying to you about your prayer life? WDYS?

He is My Father

1 John

WDYS in the Scriptures

I CAME TO KNOW the Lord when I was nine years old. I didn't live with my parents, and my childhood was difficult. God, however, was always with me, kept me safe, and put people in my life who loved me. As a child I didn't understand this, but as I grew older, I came to realize how important He was in my life. He has always been my father. He is the only father I have ever known. On Father's Day, I was never sad because I knew I had the best father in the world.

Many times during quiet times and prayer, He has called me His daughter. When I realize the significance of being His daughter, it brings me to tears. The one who created me is my Father and He loves me.

Our culture has many broken families, broken relationships, and broken hearts. Some fathers have been absent and left large scars on their children. Many don't want to think of Jesus as their Father because they can't relate to Him as being good if they do. We sing a song in our church called *Good, Good Father*. He is the best father. He is a very good father who loves us with an unconditional love that requires nothing back. He loves you just because you exist. He wants you to know Him and love Him back as His sons and daughters.

1 John 3:1 NLT

See how very much our Father loves us, for
he calls us his children, and that is what we

are! But the people who belong to this world don't recognize that we are God's children because they don't know him.

Do you know Jesus as your Father? Do you understand that He loves you unconditionally? You do not have to perform for Him. All He asks is that you believe He is who He says He is and accept Him as your Savior. Once you believe, you can't help but introduce others to Him because He will become the best thing you have ever experienced. What is He saying to your heart right now? WDYS?

_____

_____

_____

_____

_____

_____

_____

_____

_____

_____

_____

_____

_____

_____

DAY FIFTY-TWO

The Potter

Jeremiah 18
WDYS in the Scriptures

I WAS PRIVILEGED TO work in a busy law office in my hometown for many years. One day, I had a particularly difficult day. At home that evening I was sitting on my bed crying out to the Lord because I was upset over the circumstances of the day. Then, I started reading in Jeremiah about the potter and the clay.

Jesus spoke to my heart about how He was the one who created me, formed me, and was making me into a person (pot) which pleased Him. Although my day was a tough one, He reminded me that He was always with me and that He knew what He was doing. His formation would be what I needed, and I was to trust Him as my potter.

Sometimes being a believer is not an easy road to travel. It can have very fulfilling days and very difficult days. When we read the Word about Paul and the shipwrecks, prisons, beatings, and arrests, what room do we have to complain about a difficult day? All of God's children face difficult times. In fact, the Bible tells us that we *will* have difficult times. But, it also tells us that He will be with us through them all—just like He was with me during that particular time in my life.

He is my potter. He can form and reform me anyway He wants. There are times when I need to be back on the potter's wheel and there are times when I am pliable and in His perfect hands.

Jeremiah 18:4 NIV

But the pot he was shaping from the clay was
marred in his hands; so the potter formed it
into another pot, shaping it as seemed best
to him.

Are you willing to be on the potter's wheel so Jesus can form you into
who He desires you to become? Sometimes it can be painful, but the lessons
we learn as we are being formed lead us to our next level with Him. It is so
worth it to allow Him to make you into what seems best for Him. Is He
speaking to you today? WDYS?

DAY FIFTY-THREE

My Provider

Philippians 4
WDYS in the Scriptures

SO MANY TIMES, GOD provided for my needs, and I can't begin to even explain how it happened. My husband and I live a modest lifestyle. We have been blessed to always have what we needed. When my children reached high school and began making decisions about their futures, we prayed asking God to help us with college expenses and other needs that would accompany college.

Our daughter decided to go to a college about a half hour away. She was so excited to play college softball and room with her best friend! My husband and I trusted God and somehow were able to make all the payments for her to go to school. I wish I could tell you how we got the money, but honestly, I do not know! God simply provided all we needed for her to finish her BSN and to launch her into her career.

Four years later our son went to a Bible college in California. Because God had provided for our daughter, we knew He would also provide for our son. God never left us hungry, broke, or destitute. He is a God of provision.

If there is one thing I have learned, it is that God's Word is more concrete than anything else we stand upon. What God says, God will do. We cannot pick and choose what we believe. We believe it all, because every Word is true.

Philippians 4:19 NKJV
¹⁹ And my God shall supply all your need

according to His riches in glory by Christ
Jesus.

God supplies us not only with our physical needs, but also our emotional and spiritual needs. You can trust Him with it all. What is He speaking to your heart today? Do you trust Him to meet your needs? Talk with Him and then write down what He shares with you. WDYS?

_____

_____

_____

_____

_____

_____

_____

_____

_____

_____

_____

_____

_____

_____

_____

_____

Let It Go

Matthew 6

WDYS in the Scriptures

IN MATTHEW 6, JESUS was asked how to pray. What we now call the Lord's Prayer follows. Verse 12 teaches us to ask for forgiveness of our sins and guarantees He will forgive us. But Jesus wasn't done there. In verses 14 and 15, He goes on to teach that when we forgive others, our heavenly Father will forgive us. When we don't forgive others, neither will we be forgiven.

This passage reminds me of a situation I was in not that long ago. Someone had done something to me, thinking I didn't know it, but I did. Every time I saw that person or even heard their name, I was immediately filled with judgmental thoughts toward that person. One day during my quiet time with the Lord, He dealt with me. He told me that if I didn't forgive this person, I would go no further in my walk with Him.

You see, we really don't have a choice. We are commanded to forgive others. Forgiveness does not mean that we have to be best friends with that person again. However, it does mean that we must let it go. We give it to God, and every time that thought runs through our mind again, we give it to Him again and forgive them. One day when we pass that person in the store, we will no longer have that feeling in the pit of our stomach because we have fully forgiven them.

If you want a victorious walk with Jesus, you must forgive and let go of anything that you are holding on to. It is not a suggestion. It is the key to living in harmony with others and in obedience with the Father.

Matthew 6:7–15 NKJV

[7] "And when you pray, do not use vain repetitions as the heathen do. For they think that they will be heard for their many words. [8] Therefore do not be like them. For your Father knows the things you have need of before you ask Him. [9] In this manner, therefore, pray:

> Our Father in heaven,
> Hallowed be Your name.
> [10] Your Kingdom come.
> Your will be done
> On earth as it is in heaven.
> [11] Give us this day our daily bread,
> [12] And forgive us our debts,
> As we forgive our debtors.
> [13] And do not lead us into temptation,
> But deliver us from the evil one.
> For Yours is the kingdom and the
> power and the glory forever. Amen.

[14] For if you forgive men their trespasses, your heavenly Father will also forgive you. [15] But if you do not forgive men their trespasses, neither will your Father forgive your trespasses."

I am thankful that God called me on the carpet regarding this offense. I now walk in freedom and forgiveness. Who do you need to forgive today? What do you see in your life that needs to be shared with Jesus? WDYS?

_____

_____

_____

_____

The Command with A Promise

Malachi

WDYS in the Scriptures

I WAS TAUGHT AS a young teenager to tithe or give to the church 10 percent of all my income. A tithe provides the church with the needed finances to pay the expenses of the church. Tithing also allows a church to give to other ministries and help people in need. Our tithe can be used by God to touch our neighbors and friends, meeting needs that are unknown to us.

I know people who tithe on gift cards and birthday money. Some even give more than 10 percent of their income. God teaches that He owns everything that we have. He commands that we give 10 percent of what we earn to Him. At times, giving that tithe was difficult, but we were obedient to His Word and gave it anyway. As I sit here writing this today and look around, I can see blessing after blessing that Jesus has given us.

When we are obedient in tithing, we are given a promise that we will be blessed. I love promises from God, because He is a promise keeper. Even more, I love promises that carry a blessing for obedience. I have never missed a payment or gone hungry for a day because of His provision.

Malachi 3:10–12 NLT

[10] "Bring all the tithes into the storehouse so
there will be enough food in my Temple. If
you do," says the LORD of Heaven's Armies,
"I will open the windows of heaven for you.
I will pour out a blessing so great you won't

have enough room to take it in! Try it! Put me to the test! [11] Your crops will be abundant, for I will guard them from insects and disease. Your grapes will not fall from the vine before they are ripe," says the LORD of Heaven's Armies. [12] "Then all nations will call you blessed, for your land will be such a delight," says the LORD of Heaven's Armies.

This is a promise that is worth checking out. Do you tithe to your church? Do you think you can't afford your bills if you tithe? Tithing is a heart condition. Do you trust God to take care of you? I challenge you to put God first and be obedient to His Word. Become a tither and watch Him bless you in return. What is He showing you today about tithing? WDYS?

_____

_____

_____

_____

_____

_____

_____

_____

_____

_____

_____

_____

_____

DAY FIFTY-SIX

Trust
Proverbs 3
WDYS in the Scriptures

PROVERBS 3 TEACHES US that we are to trust in the Lord with all our heart. That means when uncertain times come, and they will, that we go directly to Him and trust in only Him. We often trust our jobs, families, bank accounts, other people, and even ourselves. This scripture teaches us not to trust in our own understanding.

Why would Jesus say that? Because our understanding comes from our mind and our minds don't think like He does. Only God knows tomorrow. Only God has our best interests at heart. Only God can make things happen. We can try, but ultimately the outcome is in His hands. I learned that when I trusted in my own understanding I fell terribly short of accomplishing my goals.

Trusting in God has seen me through many difficult times. He has provided me with jobs, finances, a home, children, food, clothing, and family, and I could fill this page with more. It is wisdom to trust in Him, and it is unwise not to. When we trust in Him, He will direct our paths. Who else would you want to give you direction?

Proverbs 3:5–6 NKJV

⁵ Trust in the LORD with all your heart,
And lean not on your own understanding;
⁶ In all your ways acknowledge Him,
And He shall direct your paths.

We live in a culture where people contact mediums, use Ouija boards, read their daily horoscope, and use tarot cards to find out what they should do with their lives. Would you rather trust a board with unknown spirits attached to it or a God who knows everything about you? The answer is obvious. Who do you trust? When we trust our heavenly Father, He will direct us in the way we should go. Is Jesus speaking to you about where you place your trust? Trust in Him. Write down what He is showing you today. WDYS?

_____

_____

_____

_____

_____

_____

_____

_____

_____

_____

_____

_____

_____

_____

_____

DAY FIFTY-SEVEN

Healer

1 Peter

WDYS in the Scriptures

JESUS IS MY HEALER. When we consider the cross, we know that He died for our sins. But the power of the cross is not only for our salvation, it is also for our healing. Jesus suffered greatly prior to His death so we would know Him and be healed by His stripes on the cross.

I can't begin to count the number of times that I have prayed for healing not only for myself but for many others. Healing is part of the atonement. We qualify for healing when we accept Jesus as our Savior. There are many stories in the Bible about healing. One of my favorite phrases in the Gospels is "...and He healed them all." He didn't pick and choose who was going to be healed. He healed everyone brought to Him.

This belief always brings up the question of "then why wasn't my family member healed?" I wish I had the answer for that question. My only response is that Jesus is sovereign and I trust that the decisions He makes are within His will. Regardless of whether everyone is healed, I believe that God still heals today. I have been healed, family members have been healed, and I have faith to believe in healing for all those I pray for. I trust God with His answer.

1 Peter 2:24 NIV

"He himself bore our sins" in his body on the
cross, so that we might die to sins and live
for righteousness; "by his wounds you have
been healed."

Do you need healing today? Do you know someone who needs healing? We live in a dark, depraved world where sin runs rampant. Because of that, illnesses are among us. I encourage you to engage your faith and believe that you or your friend will receive healing in the name of Jesus. What is Jesus saying to you about healing? Write it down. WDYS?

_____

_____

_____

_____

_____

_____

_____

_____

_____

_____

_____

_____

_____

_____

_____

_____

Protector

Psalm 91

WDYS in the Scriptures

WHEN I THINK ABOUT Jesus being my protector, I am taken back to when I was around ten years old and walking home alone from school. At the end of the road, next to a wooded area, was a car with a man inside. He was alone in his car doing inappropriate things (although I had no idea at the time what he was doing). He motioned for me to come over to him. I ignored him and went straight home.

I believe God protected me that day from what could have been a terrible offense. God protects us often when we are not aware of it. He has kept us safe in the car when cars around us are going in wrong directions. He has protected us from illnesses. He has protected our jobs and our home. He has protected our children in cars and on ballfields. I could list numerous times that God has protected me and my family. He is my protector.

Psalm 91 NLT

¹ Those who live in the shelter of the Most High
will find rest in the shadow of the Almighty.
² This I declare about the LORD:
He alone is my refuge, my place of safety;
he is my God, and I trust him.
³ For he will rescue you from every trap
and protect you from deadly disease.
⁴ He will cover you with his feathers.

He will shelter you with his wings.
His faithful promises are your armor and protection.
⁵ Do not be afraid of the terrors of the night,
nor the arrow that flies in the day.
⁶ Do not dread the disease that stalks in darkness,
nor the disaster that strikes at midday.
⁷ Though a thousand fall at your side,
though ten thousand are dying around you,
these evils will not touch you.
⁸ Just open your eyes,
and see how the wicked are punished.

⁹ If you make the LORD your refuge,
if you make the Most High your shelter,
¹⁰ no evil will conquer you;
no plague will come near your home.
¹¹ For he will order his angels
to protect you wherever you go.
¹² They will hold you up with their hands
so you won't even hurt your foot on a stone.
¹³ You will trample upon lions and cobras;
you will crush fierce lions and serpents under your feet!
¹⁴ The LORD says, "I will rescue those who love me.
I will protect those who trust in my name.
¹⁵ When they call on me, I will answer;
I will be with them in trouble.
I will rescue and honor them.
¹⁶ I will reward them with a long life
and give them my salvation."

This Psalm shows how much God loves and cares for us. I remember reading it to my children on September 11, 2001, when the World Trade Center was attacked. It brought great comfort in a very difficult time. His protection is available to us every day. What is God saying to you about his protection? WDYS?

_____

_____

_____

_____

_____

_____

_____

_____

_____

_____

_____

_____

_____

_____

_____

_____

_____

_____

Be Teachable

Matthew 5

WDYS in the Scriptures

I HAVE KNOWN MEN and women who believe they know everything already and do not need to be taught anything. This is a dangerous position to be in. When we are not teachable, we cannot see or hear important information that is vital to our life.

The Bible is full of teachers, priests, prophets, disciples, and followers of God who taught others how to understand the things of God. Knowing God is a journey that begins at salvation and ends when we are called home to heaven. The Word says that we know in part now, but when we see Him face to face, we will see clearly.

I have learned many things over my lifetime. The biggest thing I have learned is that I have a lot to learn. The more we know, the more we understand that we don't know much. (Read that again slowly.) One of the many things I have learned is that I need to be teachable.

In Matthew, Jesus climbs up on the mountain and begins to teach the multitudes that followed Him all about the Kingdom of God. Jesus is the King of the Kingdom. When we follow Him and His teachings, we become partakers in the Kingdom of God. Matthew 5–7 is known as the Sermon on the Mount. This is where He lays it all out and teaches the people about His kingdom. If we want to learn how to follow Jesus, we need to read these chapters in Matthew. When I read these chapters, I am often convicted when God points out areas in my life that need improvement.

Keeping a teachable heart throughout our journey will enable God to show us our errors and help us make necessary course corrections. He is never cruel or rude, rather He is consistent, patient, and leads us out of our sin and into His righteousness.

Matthew 5:1–2 NKJV
¹ And seeing the multitudes, He went up on a mountain, and when He was seated His disciples came to Him. ² Then He opened His mouth and taught them, saying:

As you can see, I stopped the verse early. That is because it begins the Beatitudes and is followed by the rest of the Sermon on the Mount. It is our responsibility to learn about Him so we know who He is. Do you know who Jesus is? Do you want to know Him more? Be teachable. Before you read the Word, ask Him to lead you and help you understand what He is teaching. He will teach you. What is He speaking to your heart? Write it down.

_____

_____

_____

_____

_____

_____

_____

_____

_____

_____

DAY SIXTY

Promise Keeper

Psalm 113

WDYS in the Scriptures

WHEN MY HUSBAND AND I had been married for around three years, we decided that we wanted to start a family. As time went on and we didn't get pregnant, I went to the doctor who was treating me medically.

During this time, we went to our church camp as counselors for the junior high children. I was in ministry at the end of a service. A prophecy was given which I didn't hear because I was distracted by praying for the youth. A pastor who heard the prophecy came to me after the service and told me that I would get pregnant and have children. The verse I received was Psalm 113:9. I held that scripture before the Lord from that time forward.

After waiting for what seemed like forever, I gave birth to our first baby, a daughter. Four years later we had our son. We were married almost ten years before we had our first child. God always keeps His promises. It may not be in the timetable we would like, rather it is in His timetable. His timing is always perfect!!

Our children are now grown and have children of their own. We have five grandchildren. God has truly blessed our lives. He has never failed me. His promises are true, and we are guaranteed that He will always fulfill what He says He will do!

Psalm 113:9 NIV

He settles the childless woman in her home

as a happy mother of children.
Praise the LORD.

The Word of God is the only thing in our lives that is guaranteed. Everything we read in the Bible is true. When we put our trust in Him, we can trust that His promises are true. Just as the good promises about eternal life with the Father are true so are the ones concerning eternal life without Him. If you have friends or family or know people who need Jesus, please don't stop praying for them and witnessing to them about His great love. He wants all His kids in heaven with Him. WDYS?

DAY SIXTY-ONE

Dreams
Psalm 37
WDYS in the Scriptures

As a young girl, I always dreamed of going into the ministry. Having been raised in a foster home, I did not have the finances to go to college. In high school I studied to be a stenographer so I could provide for myself. Following graduation, I went straight to work.

After getting married, we settled down in a new state and found jobs. I began attending the church where God planted me, and I began to help out in any area I could. Years later, to further my education and be more equipped to teach, I became credentialed in my church. Soon after that, I met a pastor who was a professor in a Bible college. I was given the opportunity to attend classes, and a few years later, I obtained my associate's degree in ministry.

I retired from a secular job after thirty years and then began full time ministry. The privilege of helping our Senior Pastor and working in ministry is a dream that the Lord allowed me to fulfill. However, I don't serve God only within the confines of the church. We are called to make disciples of all people. We serve God outside the church as well. Jesus will use anyone who loves Him, credentialed or not, to talk to others about Him. Never miss an opportunity to tell someone about Jesus!

When you delight yourself in the Lord, He truly gives you the desires of your heart.

Psalm 37:4 NKJV
Delight yourself also in the LORD, And He
shall give you the desires of your heart.

Do you have an unfulfilled desire in your heart? Do you have dreams that are not accomplished? There are ways to make your dreams come true. Pray about it and trust God to show you how. This book is a dream that is coming true right now. God has allowed me to meet the right people to accomplish this dream. You can too. WDYS?

_____

_____

_____

_____

_____

_____

_____

_____

_____

_____

_____

_____

_____

_____

_____

_____

DAY SIXTY-TWO

Faithful

Deuteronomy 31
WDYS in the Scripture

HAVE YOU WONDERED IF you were the only one who felt the way you do or that you are really different from everyone else? I have felt like that many times. I have felt as though I didn't fit in, causing me to feel very uncomfortable. I have often asked myself what was wrong with me because I saw things so differently.

One day at work, an incident occurred which resulted in a difference of opinion about a project. I was concerned about the impact of that decision. That evening, I prayed about what had occurred, and the Lord showed me that I did not need to fear man. He told me that He had my back and to continue to stand for Him and He would protect me. I got up the next morning believing what the Lord said and went to work. Just as He promised, all things worked out for my good.

At times, we might need to take a stand as believers that others will not understand. The position we take could even have potential to change relationships. Even so, we must be prepared to stand up for what we believe.

God is faithful to always be who He is. He can't be anything else. When I have needed Him to fight for me, He has. When I have been hurt, He has calmed me down. When I am afraid, He is there to comfort me. And when I rejoice, He is there too. He has always been by my side, just as He is always by your side.

Deuteronomy 31:6 NKJV

Be strong and of good courage, do not fear
nor be afraid of them; for the LORD your
God, He is the One who goes with you. He
will not leave you nor forsake you.

Have people abandoned you in your life? Have you felt different, alone
or uncomfortable in certain situations? Remember His Word. "I will never
leave you." You can find that verse again in Hebrews 13:5. He had it written
down twice so that we wouldn't forget. WDYS?

_____

_____

_____

_____

_____

_____

_____

_____

_____

_____

_____

_____

_____

_____

DAY SIXTY-THREE

Be Still and Know

Psalm 46

WDYS in the Scripture

I WAS ONCE CHALLENGED to pick a scripture and meditate on it in my heart. I was to copy it and put it in places where I could see it all the time. I was to pray about it. This scripture soon became what I spoke about, what I thought about, and what I began to structure my life around.

I am the type of person who wants to dive headfirst into whatever project is before me. There were times I didn't take enough time to really think a project through and get my thoughts together. Sometimes it caused me to have to backpedal or undo things I had done.

Charging ahead of God's timing and doing it by ourselves will cause many heartaches. When we do that, we are telling God that we've got this and that we don't need Him. That way of thinking is wrong and will cause many trip ups! Be still, be still, be still—this was whispered in my ear many times by God. Many times, I had to turn around, sit down, and wait on Him.

The good news is that now I love to wait on Him because I know His plan is far greater than mine and He knows what He is doing. It involves trust and acceptance of His plans and His timing. I have learned to be still and let God do what He does. When I do, I often find that I am just along for the ride. I love that!

Psalm 46:10 NKJV

Be still, and know that I am God;

I will be exalted among the nations,
I will be exalted in the earth!

Are you a take charge kind of person? Be careful. Remember to be still or stop and listen to what God is saying first. It is important for the success of what you are trying to accomplish to be still and listen to Him before you dive in. There will be a sense of satisfaction in doing it God's way. He whispers, "Be still, and check with me first." WDYS?

_____

_____

_____

_____

_____

_____

_____

_____

_____

_____

_____

_____

_____

_____

_____

DAY SIXTY-FOUR

What Do You See Now

Titus 2
WDYS in the Scripture

WHEN I STARTED THIS journey, God told me to write down what He showed me. I never even imagined writing it in a book. But here it is.

I do believe Titus 2 tells us that the older are to teach the younger. The mature believers have made many mistakes. The purpose is not to make the younger feel inferior. Rather, it is to protect them and bring them into maturity sooner so they can begin to mentor the younger sooner. Also, it isn't just about age. It is about where we are in our walk with the Lord. We can be mentored by a twenty-year-old mature believer when we are sixty. Age is irrelevant. Maturity is relevant.

Again, my prayer for you is that you begin to see Jesus every day in your life. These experiences have led me to where I am today. I want to keep learning, growing, experiencing, and seeing God in new ways. I want this relationship to always be new and exciting as I live every one of my days knowing Him.

The last section of this book is blank pages for you to begin your own journey. Will you take the challenge? Start looking for Jesus in your everyday life and in obscure places. Journal what He shows you. It will then be recorded for the future.

Thank you for reading my devotional/journal. If it has ministered to you in any way, please share it with others. My heart is that everyone sees Jesus every day in their lives!

Titus 2:1–5 NKJV

1 But as for you, speak the things which are proper for sound doctrine: 2 that the older men be sober, reverent, temperate, sound in faith, in love, in patience; 3 the older women likewise, that they be reverent in behavior, not slanderers, not given to much wine, teachers of good things— 4 that they admonish the young women to love their husbands, to love their children, 5 to be discreet, chaste, homemakers, good, obedient to their own husbands, that the word of God may not be blasphemed.

What does this scripture reveal to your heart about teaching others? We teach others everyday about our Jesus by the way we live our lives. What is Jesus speaking to your heart right now? WDYS?

_____

_____

_____

_____

_____

_____

_____

_____

_____

MY JOURNEY

Start Date: _____

Date: _____

Prayer

FATHER, I THANK YOU for this new day. I thank you for waking me up and getting me out of bed. I am giving you back this day which you have given me. Today I ask that you reveal Yourself to me in new ways. Let me see you everywhere I go. My desire is to grow closer to you today. I invite you to whisper in my ear. Amen.

What Did You See Today?

Date: _____

Prayer

FATHER, I THANK YOU for this new day. I thank you for waking me up and getting me out of bed. I am giving you back this day which you have given me. Today I ask that you reveal Yourself to me in new ways. Let me see you everywhere I go. My desire is to grow closer to you today. I invite you to whisper in my ear. Amen.

What Did You See Today?

_____

_____

_____

_____

_____

_____

_____

_____

_____

_____

_____

_____

_____

_____

Date: _____

Prayer

FATHER, I THANK YOU for this new day. I thank you for waking me up and getting me out of bed. I am giving you back this day which you have given me. Today I ask that you reveal Yourself to me in new ways. Let me see you everywhere I go. My desire is to grow closer to you today. I invite you to whisper in my ear. Amen.

What Did You See Today?

_____

_____

_____

_____

_____

_____

_____

_____

_____

_____

_____

_____

_____

Date: _____

Prayer

FATHER, I THANK YOU for this new day. I thank you for waking me up and getting me out of bed. I am giving you back this day which you have given me. Today I ask that you reveal Yourself to me in new ways. Let me see you everywhere I go. My desire is to grow closer to you today. I invite you to whisper in my ear. Amen.

What Did You See Today?

_____

_____

_____

_____

_____

_____

_____

_____

_____

_____

_____

_____

_____

_____

Date: _____

Prayer

FATHER, I THANK YOU for this new day. I thank you for waking me up and getting me out of bed. I am giving you back this day which you have given me. Today I ask that you reveal Yourself to me in new ways. Let me see you everywhere I go. My desire is to grow closer to you today. I invite you to whisper in my ear. Amen.

What Did You See Today?

_____

_____

_____

_____

_____

_____

_____

_____

_____

_____

_____

_____

_____

Date: _____

Prayer

FATHER, I THANK YOU for this new day. I thank you for waking me up and getting me out of bed. I am giving you back this day which you have given me. Today I ask that you reveal Yourself to me in new ways. Let me see you everywhere I go. My desire is to grow closer to you today. I invite you to whisper in my ear. Amen.

What Did You See Today?

_____

_____

_____

_____

_____

_____

_____

_____

_____

_____

_____

_____

_____

_____

Date: _____

Prayer

FATHER, I THANK YOU for this new day. I thank you for waking me up and getting me out of bed. I am giving you back this day which you have given me. Today I ask that you reveal Yourself to me in new ways. Let me see you everywhere I go. My desire is to grow closer to you today. I invite you to whisper in my ear. Amen.

What Did You See Today?

Date: _____

Prayer

FATHER, I THANK YOU for this new day. I thank you for waking me up and getting me out of bed. I am giving you back this day which you have given me. Today I ask that you reveal Yourself to me in new ways. Let me see you everywhere I go. My desire is to grow closer to you today. I invite you to whisper in my ear. Amen.

What Did You See Today?

_____

_____

_____

_____

_____

_____

_____

_____

_____

_____

_____

_____

_____

Date: _____

Prayer

FATHER, I THANK YOU for this new day. I thank you for waking me up and getting me out of bed. I am giving you back this day which you have given me. Today I ask that you reveal Yourself to me in new ways. Let me see you everywhere I go. My desire is to grow closer to you today. I invite you to whisper in my ear. Amen.

What Did You See Today?

_____

_____

_____

_____

_____

_____

_____

_____

_____

_____

_____

_____

_____

Date: _____

Prayer

FATHER, I THANK YOU for this new day. I thank you for waking me up and getting me out of bed. I am giving you back this day which you have given me. Today I ask that you reveal Yourself to me in new ways. Let me see you everywhere I go. My desire is to grow closer to you today. I invite you to whisper in my ear. Amen.

What Did You See Today?

_____

_____

_____

_____

_____

_____

_____

_____

_____

_____

_____

_____

_____

Date: _____

Prayer

FATHER, I THANK YOU for this new day. I thank you for waking me up and getting me out of bed. I am giving you back this day which you have given me. Today I ask that you reveal Yourself to me in new ways. Let me see you everywhere I go. My desire is to grow closer to you today. I invite you to whisper in my ear. Amen.

What Did You See Today?

_____

_____

_____

_____

_____

_____

_____

_____

_____

_____

_____

_____

_____

_____

Date: _____

Prayer

FATHER, I THANK YOU for this new day. I thank you for waking me up and getting me out of bed. I am giving you back this day which you have given me. Today I ask that you reveal Yourself to me in new ways. Let me see you everywhere I go. My desire is to grow closer to you today. I invite you to whisper in my ear. Amen.

What Did You See Today?

_____

_____

_____

_____

_____

_____

_____

_____

_____

_____

_____

_____

_____

_____

Date: _____

Prayer

FATHER, I THANK YOU for this new day. I thank you for waking me up and getting me out of bed. I am giving you back this day which you have given me. Today I ask that you reveal Yourself to me in new ways. Let me see you everywhere I go. My desire is to grow closer to you today. I invite you to whisper in my ear. Amen.

What Did You See Today?

_____

_____

_____

_____

_____

_____

_____

_____

_____

_____

_____

_____

Date: _____

Prayer

FATHER, I THANK YOU for this new day. I thank you for waking me up and getting me out of bed. I am giving you back this day which you have given me. Today I ask that you reveal Yourself to me in new ways. Let me see you everywhere I go. My desire is to grow closer to you today. I invite you to whisper in my ear. Amen.

What Did You See Today?

_____

_____

_____

_____

_____

_____

_____

_____

_____

_____

_____

_____

_____

Date: _____

Prayer

FATHER, I THANK YOU for this new day. I thank you for waking me up and getting me out of bed. I am giving you back this day which you have given me. Today I ask that you reveal Yourself to me in new ways. Let me see you everywhere I go. My desire is to grow closer to you today. I invite you to whisper in my ear. Amen.

What Did You See Today?

_____

_____

_____

_____

_____

_____

_____

_____

_____

_____

_____

_____

_____

Date: _____

Prayer

FATHER, I THANK YOU for this new day. I thank you for waking me up and getting me out of bed. I am giving you back this day which you have given me. Today I ask that you reveal Yourself to me in new ways. Let me see you everywhere I go. My desire is to grow closer to you today. I invite you to whisper in my ear. Amen.

What Did You See Today?

_____

_____

_____

_____

_____

_____

_____

_____

_____

_____

_____

_____

_____

Date: _____

Prayer

FATHER, I THANK YOU for this new day. I thank you for waking me up and getting me out of bed. I am giving you back this day which you have given me. Today I ask that you reveal Yourself to me in new ways. Let me see you everywhere I go. My desire is to grow closer to you today. I invite you to whisper in my ear. Amen.

What Did You See Today?

_____

_____

_____

_____

_____

_____

_____

_____

_____

_____

_____

_____

_____

Date: _____

Prayer

FATHER, I THANK YOU for this new day. I thank you for waking me up and getting me out of bed. I am giving you back this day which you have given me. Today I ask that you reveal Yourself to me in new ways. Let me see you everywhere I go. My desire is to grow closer to you today. I invite you to whisper in my ear. Amen.

What Did You See Today?

_____

_____

_____

_____

_____

_____

_____

_____

_____

_____

_____

_____

_____

_____

Date: _____

Prayer

FATHER, I THANK YOU for this new day. I thank you for waking me up and getting me out of bed. I am giving you back this day which you have given me. Today I ask that you reveal Yourself to me in new ways. Let me see you everywhere I go. My desire is to grow closer to you today. I invite you to whisper in my ear. Amen.

What Did You See Today?

_____

_____

_____

_____

_____

_____

_____

_____

_____

_____

_____

_____

_____

Date: _____

Prayer

FATHER, I THANK YOU for this new day. I thank you for waking me up and getting me out of bed. I am giving you back this day which you have given me. Today I ask that you reveal Yourself to me in new ways. Let me see you everywhere I go. My desire is to grow closer to you today. I invite you to whisper in my ear. Amen.

What Did You See Today?

_____

_____

_____

_____

_____

_____

_____

_____

_____

_____

_____

_____

_____